Bell

Tomorrow's Child

TOMORROW'S CHILD

Imagination,
Creativity,
and the
Rebirth of Culture

Rubem A. Alves

Harper & Row, Publishers
New York, Evanston, San Francisco, London

FIRST EDITION

LIBRARY OF CONGRESS CATALOG CARD NUMBER: 77–183637

6-19-73

"All men have stars," said the little prince, "but they are not the same things for different people. For some, who are travelers, the stars are guides. For others they are no more than little lights in the sky. For others, who are scholars, they are problems. For my businessman they were wealth. But all these stars are silent. You—you alone—will have the stars as no one else has them—

"In one of the stars I shall be living. In one of them I shall be laughing. And so it will be as if all the stars were laughing, when you look at the sky at night. . . . You—only you —will have stars that can laugh!"

To Lidinha, Sergio, and Marcos,
who taught me about the laughing stars

Acknowledgments

If it were not for the year at Union Theological Seminary in New York City, I would not have had time to put together in words these ideas which grew out of my experience elsewhere in the world during these last years.

And if it were not for the imagination of the reader, who is not discouraged by the unavoidable problems of a book written in English by someone whose native tongue is not English, no communication would be possible.

Contents

Part 1

Rationalization,
or the Logic of the Dinosaur

This, indeed, is the bitterness of my bowels, that I can endure you neither naked or clothed, you men of today. All that is uncanny in the future and all that has ever made fugitive birds shudder is surely more comfortable and cozy than your "reality." For thus you speak: "Real we are entirely, and without belief or superstition." Unbelievable: thus I call you, for all your pride in being real.

—FRIEDRICH NIETZSCHE

For of the last stage of this cultural development it might well be truly said: "Specialists without spirit, sensualists without heart"; this nullity imagines that it has attained a level of civilization never before achieved.

—MAX WEBER

1

The Organization of the Absurd: Beyond Freedom, Dignity, and Life

We know dinosaurs only by their bones. The largest, most powerful animals to walk the earth are extinct. Their "arrogance of power" was of no use.

There is an irony here. If we had been their contemporaries, we would never have suspected that theirs would be such a sad and inglorious end. The stronger the better, we assume, in the struggle for existence. The more powerful a species is, the greater should be its chances of survival.

But this did not prove to be true. Animals of much more fragile structure, whose bodies were weaker and smaller beyond comparison are still around. But dinosaurs are nothing more than memories of one of life's experiments that failed.

The dinosaurs disappeared not because they were too weak, but because they were too strong. Their fantastic power came from a biological framework which was basically absurd, and the result was annihilation. Can you cure an insane person by making his body physically fit? Obviously not. This would add power to insanity, making it more insane still. The power gene-

1

rated by an irrational structure only tends to aggravate the very irrationality from which it springs. By adding power to the absurd one does not abolish it; on the contrary, it becomes still more hopelessly entangled in itself. Power is like a mathematical number inside a bracket. If the bracket is preceded by a minus sign, it is not possible to transform it into a plus by making the number bigger and bigger. This simply increases its negativity.

Power is a simple potentializing factor. It can never go beyond the logic of the structure that generates it. This is why dinosaurs had to die. Their "arrogance of power" entrapped them in the very absurdity of their organic structure. They were thereby made incapable of responding in different ways to the new challenges their environment presented.

Our civilization is behaving just like the dinosaur. Underneath everything it does, one finds the ultimate certainty that there is no problem that cannot be solved by means of a little more power. It is not by accident that for years detergent makers have been advertising "stronger," "faster," "more concentrated" and improved formulas. They know that these values control our collective unconscious. What is stronger must be better. Love of power has become our obsession, and power itself our sole god.

This is why our economy must be in a state of perpetual growth. Growth itself, sheer enlargement of power, is its end. One does not judge an economic system by asking what kinds of things it produces—whether it is creating happiness, or whether the houses men live in now are cozier than before. "Grown-ups love figures," remarked Saint–Exupéry.

When you tell them that you have made a new friend, they never ask you any questions about essential matters. They never say to you "What does his voice sound like? What games does he love best? Does he collect butterflies?" Instead they demand: "How old is he? How many brothers has he? How much does he weigh? How much money does his father make?" If you were to say to the grown-ups: "I saw a beautiful house made of rosy brick, with geraniums in the windows and doves on the roof," they would not be able to get any idea of that house at all. You would have to say to them: "I saw a house that cost $20,000." Then they would exclaim: "Oh, what a pretty house that is!"[1]

This is not a poetic exaggeration. We have been taught that efficacy is the only thing that matters, and our society functions as if it were so. How do we know if the country is all right? Where does one takes its pulse? At Wall Street. A nation is healthy if it is wealthy. More precisely: it is happy when it is rich, as an advertisement in *Newsweek* magazine suggested.

A big family? Sales last year exceeded $1.4 billion.
A growing family? Our earnings have nearly doubled in the last six years.
Needless to say: a happy family.[2]

For all practical purposes what cannot be reduced to a number does not exist for economics. This is why the quality of life produced by a given economic system does not matter at all. A "healthy economy" is a "growing economy." Whether this growth results from sales of cigarettes—of weapons, roses, or Bibles—is totally irrelevant. The important issue is not how the profit is made but rather how much profit is made. Conversely, once you reduce a life situation to a number, it loses its real quality and comes to be considered only as a good or bad investment. War, the selling of weapons, and the production of napalm are excellent investments. The death market is inexhaustible. Slave labor and *apartheid* are also good invest-

1. Antoine de Saint–Exupéry, *The Little Prince* (1943), pp. 16–17.
2. The Cities Service Company, *Newsweek* magazine, March 17, 1969. Quoted by T. Richard Snyder in (Ph.D. diss., Princeton Theological Seminary), p. 98.

ments. They produce cheap labor, and this is good for the economy. But peace and justice are bad investments. If you have any doubts, just check the national budgets and see how much is allotted to peace and how much to destruction. The prophets denounce the connection between the healthy economy and death. Businessmen reply by showing how well they are doing and how much the GNP has grown as the result of their operations. "The increase in value of the world of things increases in direct relation to the devaluation of the human world."

The same is true of the logic of war. It has a single purpose: power, sheer power. This is one of the most shocking revelations of the Pentagon Papers. There they are, the professionals of war! Their eyes and minds are turned to a situation which is filled with suffering, death, and despair. But they do not feel the suffering. They do not mention the corpses. They do not see the despair. As with the economy, the logic of war is concerned only with a systemic result: the increase of power. If love of power becomes the ultimate concern of a system, all questions about values must be dropped. Power becomes more important than life, while life is reduced to a mere means of power. Then the only questions raised are where, when, and how to exercise power.

This is how the dinosaur operated. His logic was remarkably similar to that of modern pragmatism. Both in effect keep repeating: "I need not worry about the whole—the whole will take care of itself." One takes for granted the basic structure and moves on to develop its size, power, and efficacy to the utmost limits. If something does not function well, it is because the system has not increased its power to the proper level at that point. Like the dinosaur, we ignore the fact that if the basic system is irrational and structurally faulty, greater power only accentuates its condition. As a strong insane man is more dangerous than a weak one, the increase of power in a sick system can only produce unexpected forms of its own derangement and eventually its downfall.

The fundamental question of values is never raised. We refuse to criticize the foundations upon which our civilization is built, because we simply assume that they are all right. We do not want to become radicals—indeed, this word has acquired an almost obscene connotation; we have forgotten that to be radical means simply to go to the root of things.

Once one accepts the premise that a healthy economy is in a state of perpetual growth, the only question that remains is the pragmatic one: How can we make it operate effectively? And once under the spell of this *how*, consciousness becomes incapable of looking at the foundations upon which its pragmatism is built—of asking *why?*

Unlimited growth requires a continually accelerating process of production and consumption. Goods cannot be made durable, for we must throw them away in order to buy new ones. A healthy economy requires that the logic of planned obsolescence be applied to all manufactured objects. But this creates the problem of how to dispose of them. They will have to be cast away in our space: our fields, our rivers, our seas, our air. One may hide them for a while, perhaps, by throwing everything into the bottom of the sea. But only for a while—for we live on a finite planet. As the dumping process goes on, factories must be busy making new objects. But these are not created out of nothing. One needs raw materials. Nature is plundered and ravaged. What for? To create things which will shortly become garbage. The inevitable by-product of our healthy economy is the destruction of nature. The ecological problem is not an accident. Our economy has to deliver death. The figures that indicate how fast we are growing could be used as indices of how fast the very presuppositions of life on this earth are gobbled up and destroyed. We will end by being buried in our own waste.

The same logic dominates the military mentality. The problem is no longer that of a healthy economy but "defense." It is assumed that in order to keep one's space safe one must be strong—stronger than anyone else. One must be more powerful than the enemy. It happens that the enemy thinks the same way. Power is overcome by more power, and more power by still greater power. There is no way of stopping the spiral of destructive potential in the world. But let me ask you this: Suppose the enemy attacks you with atomic weapons. You know that within a few minutes your country will be destroyed. Will you push your atomic button? That is what the logic of war demands. But what for? You will die anyway. And as you die, you will commit the ultimate act of madness; you will bring human life to an end. Why not die alone? Why not give the few who remain alive the chance of starting again? That would be so noble. But you die, and your last deed is to destroy the earth. Is it not better to have a world without you than no world at all? This seems so simple.

But suppose you answer, "We will not press the button." Then, why are you making buttons? This is insanity.

We are trapped not for lack of power, but by the unmatched effectiveness of our irrationality. We sense that we are moving toward an approaching holocaust, but feel there is nothing we can do to prevent it. Our hands are feverishly busy without our realizing that what they are doing is digging our graves. As Norman O. Brown remarked, "Mankind today is still making history without having any conscious idea of what it really wants or under what conditions it would stop being unhappy; in fact [he adds], what it is doing seems to be making itself more unhappy and calling that unhappiness progress."[4] As happened with the dinosaur, we are "possessed" by our body. And since its tendencies are basically irrational, our very efficiency commits us to the fateful results of the power logic we ourselves have created. As Rollo May once put it, we may as well prepare the epitaph for this species in danger of extinction: Man. "Like the dinosaur he had power without the ability to change, strength without the capacity to learn."[5]

This is the end of a dream and the dissolution of the very spirit that gave our civilization its life and sense of identity. We believed that the Age of Reason had arrived. This is an old hope, already fully developed in Plato's vision of the philosopher-king: "Reason is yet to become powerful. And when this day comes, the human order will be liberated from the irrational elements that disturb it, and it will then be possible to build it according to the true, the good, and the beautiful." Our culture began with the certainty that this day had arrived. As Whitehead points out, "In order to understand our epoch we can neglect all the details of change, such as railways, telegraphs, radios, spinning machines, synthetic dyes," and so on. The radical breakthrough which provided the grounds for our belief in the advent of Reason was a new method of investigation. "The greatest invention of the nineteenth century was the invention of a method of invention. A new method entered into life. That is the real novelty which has broken up the foundations of the old civilization."[6] Man discovered that it was no longer necessary to stick to the old method of moving to the future from what he already knew. Suddenly it became possible to move toward what he *wished* to know.

The revolutionary element in this shift lies in the fact that

4. Norman O. Brown, *Life Against Death* (1959), p. 16.
5. Rollo May, *Man's Search for Himself* (1953), p. 20.
6. Alfred N. Whitehead, *Science and the Modern World* (1967), p. 96.

man succeeded in making his *intention* the controlling factor of the old scientific binomial of observation + quantification—thereby putting knowledge effectively at the service of power. Although the immediate application of the method opened up new possibilities of controlling nature, its implications did not stop there. By the same logical procedures, social life as well could be brought under control. This seemed fantastic progress. If man had finally found the secret of how to shape the future according to his intentions—his desires—then the rational society was no longer simply a dream. This was the message of the Enlightenment. Science became the new Messiah—the bearer of salvation. The sorcerer's apprentice had finally realized his dream. He became the Creator's apprentice. In a letter to Walt Whitman on the occasion of his seventieth birthday, Mark Twain put into words what really became the deepest, dearest, and most universal of the certainties of our collective unconscious.

You have lived just the seventy years which are greatest in the world's history and richest in benefit and advancement to its peoples. These seventy years have done much more to widen the interval between man and the other animals than was accomplished by any of the five centuries which preceded them. What great births you have witnessed! The steam press, the steamship, the steel ship, the railroad, the perfect cotton gin, the telegraph, the phonograph, photogravure, the electrotype, the gas light, the sewing machine, and the amazing, infinitely varied and innumerable products of coal tar, those latest and strangest marvels of a marvelous age. And you have seen even greater births than these; for you have seen the application of anesthesia to surgery-practice, whereby the ancient dominion of pain, which began with the first created life, came to an end on this earth forever. . . . Yes, you have indeed seen much—but tarry for a while, for the greatest is yet to come. Wait thirty years, and *then* look out over the earth! You shall see marvels upon marvels added to those whose nativity you have witnessed; and conspicuous about them you shall see the formidable Result—man at almost his full stature at last!—and still growing, visibly growing while you look. Wait till you see that great figure appear, and catch the far glint of the sun upon his banner; then you may depart satisfied, as knowing you have seen him for whom the earth was made, and that he will proclaim that human wheat is more than human tares, and proceed to organize human values on that basis.[7]

This is the spirit of our civilization. Beneath the conscious ideological and political conflicts that divide us, we are all worshipers of the same god. Marxism, too, hails science as the savior. This is why it has been so much against the utopian socialists. According to the Marxist view it is science, or more precisely the Marxist scientific interpretation of social reality, that will open the possibilities of freedom and human fulfillment. Engels could thus recite the same creed. As a result of science, he says,

State interference in social relations becomes superfluous, and then dies out of itself; the government of persons is replaced by the administration of things. The state is not abolished; it *dies out.* . . .

The extraneous objective forces that have hitherto governed history pass under the control of man himself. Only from that time will man himself, more and more consciously, make his own history—only from that time will the social causes set in movement by him have, in the main and in a constantly growing measure, the results intended by him. . . . It is the ascent of man from the kingdom of necessity to the kingdom of freedom. Man, at last the master of his own form of social organization, becomes at the same time the lord over nature, his own master—free.[8]

The same spirit and the same confidence speak through Twain and Engels. They are two prophets who prepare the way

7. Quoted in Lewis Mumford, *The Condition of Man* (1944), pp. 305–306.
8. Friedrich Engels, *Socialism: Utopian and Scientific* (n.d.), pp. 129, 135, 139.

for a common Messiah. And the message goes on being repeated today through the mouth of the futurologues:

We are creating a new society. Not a changed society. Not an extended, longer-than-life version of our present society. But a new society. Revolution implies novelty. It sends a flood of newness into the lives of countless individuals, confronting them with unfamiliar institutions and first-time situations. Reaching deep into our personal lives, the enormous changes ahead will transform traditional family structures and sexual attitudes. They will smash conventional relationships between old and young. They will overthrow our values with respect to money and success. They will alter work, play and education beyond recognition. *And they will do all this in a context of spectacular, elegant, yet frightening scientific advance.*[9]

The ultimate result of the triumph of science, proclaims Toffler, is "the subjection of the process of evolution itself to conscious human guidance."[10]

We are told that knowledge is at the service of freedom, that technology is the handmaid of justice, and that power is under the direction of the truth. These are the basic beliefs implied in the proclamation that the Age of Reason had arrived.

There is no doubt that our society became rationalized. The problem, however, is that *rationalization is not the same thing as becoming rational* in the way we had hoped. Structures have a built-in teleology. In all of them we find one single controlling purpose. They function in order to survive. They develop efficient means to preserve themselves. This is true of organisms, of cultures, of institutions, of our psychic structure. Each one of them develops means to achieve this end. Lecky remarks that "every one's behavior is logical from his own point of view,"[11] and this statement holds true for every system. We may as well

9. Alvin Toffler, *Future Shock* (1970), p. 166. (Emphasis supplied.)
10. *Ibid.*, p. 429.
11. Prescott Lecky, *Self-Consistency: A Theory of Personality* (1961), p. 136.

rephrase it and say that *for any and every system, its functioning is logical and rational from the standpoint of the presuppositions upon which it is built.* Thus, a system considers rational
those means that make possible its continued existence.

Rationalization, therefore, does not necessarily say anything
about the values which are at its basis. As Max Weber once
pointed out, "The various great ways of leading a rational and
methodical life have been characterized by irrational presuppositions."[12] For the White minorities in South Africa the system of *apartheid* is perfectly rational. It functions. For the
businessman, the logic of the economy is rational also. It keeps
the game going. For the military, the build-up of instruments
of destruction is equally logical, since it operates on the assumption that national security requires supremacy of power.

In fact, "rationalization" has nothing to do with that hope of
a rational life which was the deepest aspiration of our civilization. The idea of Reason implied a critique of the very foundations of our social order. It had to do with justice, truth, and
goodness. It demanded conversion and regeneration. It pointed
to the need of building society upon values which were human.
Rationalization, however, totally ignores these issues and is
solely concerned with the problem of *how to make the dominant structures work—how to preserve them and increase their
power.*

Very often—indeed most of the time—we are not able to
distinguish between our *intention* in doing something and the
actual results or *function* of what we do. The intention of the
rain dance is to produce rain. But objectively it does not. Why,
then, do certain groups remain attached to the rain dance, even
if it does not deliver what it promises? The explanation is that
the ritual performs certain vital functions for the group, func-

12. Max Weber, "The Social Psychology of World Religions," in II. II. Gerth
and C. Wright Mills, eds., *From Max Weber: Essays in Sociology* (1946), p. 281.

tions of which the group itself is unaware. What is the intention of rationalization? We are told that its purpose is the "subjection of the process of evolution itself to conscious human guidance." What I am saying, however, is that this is not in fact what it accomplishes—this is not its true function.

Rationalization is not a technique for realizing the desires of our heart. It is not an instrument for making our values come true. It is not the fulfillment of Reason. The function of rationalization is the perpetuation of the systems of power—however irrational they may be—upon which our society is built. The end of every system is its own functioning. Though the realization of Reason is the confessed *intention* of our civilization, the fact is that the actual *function* of rationalization has no relation to it whatsoever. Rationalization is a function of systems of power. It is a means to make possible their perpetuation. Thus its only value is power, sheer power.

The *function* of science in our civilization has unfortunately, therefore, been quite different from its confessed *intention*. Scientists keep reciting their humanistic and even religious creeds, reassuring especially themselves that their work serves the well-being of man, but the truth of the matter is quite different. Science has become a rather expensive game. Research requires fantastic amounts of money. But science has no means to subsidize itself. Scientists know that projects must be "sold." The game of knowledge depends on the buyers. The quickest way of getting to the bottom of the matter is by simply asking science: "Who pays your bills?"

The answer is clear. Science lives to the extent that it is supported by the economic and military power systems. It has no life of its own. Alone, it cannot survive. And why do the economic and military systems "protect" and subsidize science? Systems of power function in order to increase power. They finance science only if and when it pays dividends—i.e., when it delivers what they are looking for, when it gives them know-how which makes possible the extension of their power. Paul Goodman once remarked that the simplest explanation for the proposition that we have more scientists today than during the rest of history is that economic interests have succeeded in putting science at their service. Our society has not become more scientific; rather, science has been transformed into an exploitable function.[13] In his analysis of the world of organization (which is one of the products of rationalization itself), William H. Whyte, Jr. describes very well the regrettable condition of the scientist, reduced to the status of functionary. No firm wants to subsidize the idle curiosity of its scientists. They must be helped to become "company-conscious." "Company loyalty is not only more important than idle curiosity; it helps *prevent* idle curiosity."[14] The same may be said of the relation between science and war. War has become a scientific business, and science itself has become a weapon. The need to control, to spy, and to kill provides a fantastic market for scientists anxious to sell their projects.

It is not my intention to say anything against the character of scientists. I am simply pointing out that virtuosity in problem-solving is more often than not coupled with political idiocy. The scientist assures himself that since his intentions are innocent and he is involved in the field of pure thought, the result of his work can not serve any function which is opposed to his intentions. It would be comical if it were not so tragic. As Robert Musil has pointed out, "Mathematics, the mother of the exact natural sciences, the grandmother of engineering, was also the arch-mother of that spirit from which, in the end, poison-gases and fighter aircraft have been born. Actually," he continues, "the only people living in ignorance of these dangers were the

13. Paul Goodman, "La Moralidad de la Technologia Científica."
14. William H. Whyte, Jr. *The Organization Man* (1956), pp. 229–32.

mathematicians themselves and their disciples, the natural scientists, who felt no more of all this in their soul than racing-cyclists who are pedalling away hard *with no eyes for anything in the world but the back wheel of the man in front.*"[15]

Science has a repressed unconscious. It is too hard for it to acknowledge that it is receiving blood transfusions from Mephisto; scientists would rather believe their own intentions than the bitter facts of power.

The idea of the neutrality of science and technology is no longer tenable. Power does not subsidize neutrality. Scientists believe themselves to be creators of *possibilities.* "Every possibility is neutral in itself," they say. "It is up to you to use them responsibly." I think most scientists would tend to agree with David Sarnoff: "We are too prone to make technological instruments the scapegoats for the sins of those who wield them. The products of modern science are not in themselves good or bad; it is the way they are used that determines their value."[16] Scientists explain the obvious contradiction between their confessed humanistic intentions and the actual results of their work by transferring the moral responsibility to someone else. It is an easy way of washing one's hands of it. Science is depicted as a process free of the realities of power and therefore not responsible for the use power makes of the knowledge it creates. "This is the voice of current somnambulism," says McLuhan in response to Sarnoff's statement. "Suppose we were to say, 'An apple pie is in itself neither good or bad; it is the way it is used that determines its value.' Or, 'The smallpox virus is in itself neither good or bad; it is the way it is used that determines its value.' Again, 'Firearms are in themselves neither good or bad;

15. Robert Musil, *The Man Without Qualities* (1965), p. 41. Emphasis supplied.

16. Quoted in Marshall McLuhan, *Understanding Media: The Extensions of Man* (1964), p. 11.

it is the way they are used that determines their value.' That is, if slugs reach the right people, firearms are good.' "[17]

But means which are created already have stamped on them the intention of the power structures that make their manufacture possible. They are arrows flying toward an end. Their real function, therefore, is not determined either by the humanist intention of the scientist or by the claims of the scientific community as to its objective and value-free posture. It is rather the way science is related to the dominant structures of power that determines its real function. In our society science is a function of certain power games. The unavoidable consequence of this fact is that behind the apparent variety of its accomplishments is the common denominator of everything it does: the perpetuation of the relations of power.

The greatest of all the creations of science is thus none of its isolated miracles. No one of them can account for the radically new quality of our human experience in this age. Science changed history when, by means of rationalization, it made it possible for power to fulfill its ultimate dream: the transformation of the whole world into Organization. Indeed, Organization is nothing more than the rationalization of power.

The word Organization comes from *organ*. To organize, then, is literally to transform something whose elements are unrelated, disconnected, or dysfunctional into a functional item, i.e., a means. The ideal of corporations is to transform the entire world into a unified market: same desires, same needs, same acquisitive power. This would simplify immensely all the problems involved in production. At the same time, they must organize the world's resources so as to be available to transform into goods to be consumed by the world-wide market. The ideal of the military is, equally, to organize the world so that all

17. *Ibid.*, p. 11.

disconnected units of power, represented by individual nations, will be functions of the will of the master. The "colony" is a nation which has become an organ. It has no will of its own. It does what it is told.

This was the basic principle of the Monroe Doctrine: Latin America was to have no autonomy. The same purpose was hidden behind the idea of the "protectorate" and expressed in the concept of "areas of influence." The slave is one who has ceased to be "for himself"; he has become an organ of the master. The purpose of racial segregation is to transform Blacks into functions of Whites. They (Blacks) become "organized" according to the will of the Whites. South Africa is thus a highly organized society. Behind the organizational thrust one always finds the intention to eliminate the dysfunctional and see that everyone plays the game according to the rules set up by the center of power.

Thus in our civilization, organization and freedom are self-excluding concepts. As Dewey remarked, "We live in a world in which there is an immense amount of organization, but it is an *external* organization, not one of *the ordering of a growing experience,* one that involves, moreover, the whole of the live creature, *towards a fulfilling conclusion.*"[18] Modern Organization (as I shall call this external phase) is not an expression of life. It does not grow out of it. On the contrary, it is imposed, it comes from above. In Organization we do not find the *logic of life* creating a space and a time for itself, but rather the *logic of power* transforming life into one of its own functions. And since the logic of power knows only one value—the protection and increase of power—and totally ignores the requirements of life, it is inevitable that the world of Organization conspires against life. There cannot be, therefore, any peaceful coexist-

18. John Dewey, *Art as Experience* (1958), p. 81. Emphasis supplied.

ence between the ideal of democracy and the world of Organization as it exists in our civilization.

The ideal of democracy expresses the belief that for a society to be human it has to grow out of the people's hopes and aspirations. This is why power had to belong to the people. It was a way of affirming that if Organization is to be expressive of—and instrumental to—life, then life itself has to remain in power.

In Organization, however, we do not find life organizing itself, but rather power organizing life. Power is the end. Life is a means. The logic of life is superseded by that of power.

Individuals must be organized, and this is what education is for. As Clark Kerr puts it, the university "is a factory for the production of knowledge and technicians to service society's many bureaucracies."[19] Persons must become means and functions. Behavior as an expression of the natural rhythms of the body and the aspirations of social groups must be discontinued. Individuals and communities must function as transistors in an electronic circuit: What Toffler calls the "modular" and therefore "disposable" man. What one does must be a response to the functional requirements of the whole. The Skinner box is the mini-model of this macro-world. Stimuli condition behavior, and behavior functions according to the rules of the game.

Thus Organization produces repression. Indeed, Organization *is* repression. This was perceived some time ago by one of the most lucid prophets of our era. "No special proof is necessary to show that military discipline is the ideal model for the modern capitalist factory, as it was for the ancient plantation," remarked Max Weber. "The individual is shorn of his natural rhythm as determined by the structure of his organism; his psychophysical apparatus is attuned to a new rhythm through a methodical specialization of separately functioning muscles

19. S. M. Lipset and S. S. Wolin, eds., *The Student Berkeley Revolt: Facts and Interpretations* (1965), p. 213.

and an optimal economy of forces is established corresponding to the conditions of work."

The factory is the model of what happens in the whole world. The inevitable result of "this universal phenomenon," he remarks sadly, is that it "increasingly restricts the importance of charisma and of individually differentiated conduct."[20] From the point of view of Organization, these are dysfunctional and therefore disruptive elements which must be abolished.

The rationalized society has in fact moved "beyond freedom and dignity." It has abandoned life as its ultimate value and has put power in its place. It is quite significant that Weber chose *violence* as the decisive index for defining the dominant structures of life. What characterizes the state, he says, is that it is "a community that (successfully) claims the *monopoly of the legitimate use of physical force within a given territory.*"[21] Sigmund Freud may be considered the ideologue par excellence of this state of affairs, for he not only acknowledges the rule of violence but declares it to be necessary and therefore justifiable. His firm conviction is that "it is just as impossible to do without control of the mass by a minority as it is to dispense with coercion in the work of civilization. For the masses are lazy and unintelligent; they have no love for instinctual renunciation, and they are not to be convinced by argument of its inevitability; and the individuals composing them support one another in giving free rein to their undiscipline. Every civilization," he concludes, "must be built up on coercion."[22] Beneath his moral defense of violence there lurks a profound mistrust of the wisdom of life and an unwarranted optimism as to the wisdom and disinterestedness of the elites.

20. S. N. Eisenstadt, ed., *Max Weber: On Charisma and Institution Building* (1968), pp. 38–39.
21. Gerth and Mills, *op. cit.*, p. 78.
22. *The Future of an Illusion* (1964), pp. 5–6.

I have stated that the controlling value of our systems of power is their own self-perpetuation. Moreover, they have reversed the logic of life by transforming it into a means, and power into an end. I have indicated further that the function of rationalization is not the humanization of our world but rather the creation of conditions for perpetuating the power that now governs it. Perhaps these statements did not shock the reader. When one speaks abstractly it is very easy to forget that abstraction is a way of speaking of concrete conditions of life. Abstractions seldom produce pain. Perhaps this is why George Orwell decided to preach his lesson not in the language against the background of the classroom, but through the mouth of the jailor in the sinister environment of the torture chamber.

The Party seeks power entirely for its own sake. We are not interested in the good of others; we are interested solely in power. Not wealth or luxury or long life or happiness; only power, pure power. What pure power means you will understand presently. We are different from all the oligarchies of the past in that we know what we are doing. All the others, even those who resembled ourselves, were cowards and hypocrites. The German Nazis and the Russian Communists came very close to us in their methods, but they never had the courage to recognize their own motives. They pretended, perhaps even believed, that they had seized power unwillingly and for a limited time, and that just round the corner there lay a paradise where human beings would be free and equal. We are not like that. We know that no one ever seizes power with the intention of relinquishing it. *Power is not a means; it is an end.* One does not establish a dictatorship in order to safeguard a revolution; one makes the revolution to establish the dictatorship. The object of persecution is persecution. The object of torture is torture. *The object of power is power.*[23]

Nineteen Eighty-Four is more than science fiction. It is prophecy. It talks about the insanity of the present by project-

23. *Nineteen Eighty-Four*, (1949), pp. 266–677.

ing its tendencies in their ultimate consequences upon the screen of the future. The future tense is only a parabolic way of casting light on the underground, unconscious, hidden demonic impulses already operative in our society.

The democratic dream made us believe that power is exercised either by individuals or groups of individuals. This is why one assumed that it makes a radical difference if Johnson is elected instead of Goldwater, or if the Republican party instead of the Democratic wins the power. But people are already discovering that this dream is an illusion.

"The more things change the more they remain the same." One can change at will those who seem to be in power and shift from one party to another. It makes no difference. Because those who seem to be in charge are not really in charge. They are nothing more than transistors in a network of power, executives plugged into a system. And ultimately it is the system that programs the course of operations. Individuals are expendable, disposable. Paul already knew this political reality better than we. "For our fight is not against human foes, but against cosmic powers, against authorities and potentates of this dark world, against the superhuman forces of evil in the heavens," he says (Eph. 6:12). The language is mythic and symbolic. The reality of which it speaks is hard and painful. Power is not located in individuals but in structures. The obvious is a mask of what really is. Power is invisible. Franz Kafka conveys well the weird feeling of what it means to live in its grip. One walks through the corridors and rooms of the Castle and meets many people behind desks, yet none of them is really in charge. Filling the whole atmosphere is the presence of the Lord of the Castle. But no matter how hard one tries, one never succeeds in meeting him. By becoming invisible power has put itself beyond the reach of man. It can no longer be attacked. Nowhere has man's helplessness been more obvious than in the politics of protest.

Protest is a tactic which assumes that there is someone to hear, someone to be frightened, someone to be moved. People go to the streets, ready for the great comfrontation. But it never occurs, for the simple reason that there is no one in charge behind the desks. Protest becomes a sort of punching the air, crying in the wilderness, fighting windmills. At the same time, protected by its invisibility, power controls man in a much more subtle and total way. "I can go wherever I want to. I drive my car, I watch TV, I go to supermarkets, to drive-ins, to church, to the golfclub, I travel abroad. Nobody presses me. I am alone. I am free."

Structures are not persons or things. They are not buildings. Not even organizations. Structures are global relations, and relations cannot be seen. They are to society what the mind is to the body: the controlling logic of behavior. No matter how painfully an executive is aware of the need to humanize the economy by making it responsive to human values, there is nothing he can do to change the logic of profit. For this is the dominant global relationship that governs the rules of his game. No matter how painfully aware a militarist may be of the absurdity of war, he cannot eliminate the logical presuppositions behind his uniform. The fate of Lt. Col. Anthony Herbert, 41, who charged atrocities by U.S. troops in Vietnam, is a painful evidence of this fact. When men are reduced to functionaries of global systems, there is nothing that they can do to transform them.

This, it seems to me, is the qualitatively new element characterizing our modern situation: rationalized, organized power has become invisible as never before, and has gained the highest degree of efficiency, which borders invulnerability, known in history.

What are the components of these structures that retain the monopoly of power?

First, the game of the corporations. No matter how sophisticated it may become, the fundamental fact remains: what is basically at stake here is money-making, profit, and economic domination. Without the profit motive, the game of the corporations could not be played at all. It establishes the only mode of appropriation that is admissible in the society it has organized: buying and possessing.

The economy does not move alone, however. It lives symbiotically with the game of war. They are allies. War cannot be waged without a "healthy economy" to support it. On the other hand, war is good business. It keeps factories busy. Its commodities have a sure market. In no other situation is the transient life of goods, and therefore the pace of production and consumption, so basic to our superindustrial society and so close to ideal conditions as in war. It is quite revealing that Robert McNamara moves with ease from the Pentagon to the World Bank. How is this possible? Because there is a common logical identity underlying both systems. War and the economy are two different ways of playing the same game, the game of power.

Science, on the other hand, is a parasitic game. It lives to the extent that it is plugged into the game of war and the game of the corporations. These are the sources of its life. Without them the puzzle-solving activity could not go on, and its function is to give power the brain it lacks.

Three interlocking games. A symbiotic, parasitic relationship in which each one potentializes its own power and adds greater power to its partners. Together they form a single, indivisible system with identical interests and therefore a single unifying logic. As with the dinosaur: great efficiency has been added to the absurd, and the absurd becomes the Creator and Master of the world in which we live. We actually live under the power of rationalized insanity.

2

The Child of the Absurd: The Shocking Future

The triumph of power is not a simple thing.

Slaves rebel against their masters; colonized peoples dream of independence; occupied nations sabotage the operations of the conqueror; Blacks resist Whites; women denounce men; youth refuses to obey its elders; the poor cannot avoid hating those who exploit them. The exploited will not willingly give up their aspirations, and they are not to be convinced by arguments of the inevitability of control. They resist. And by this act they become dysfunctional elements in the Organization of power and need to be eliminated in one way or another.

Resistance can be overcome by brute force. "Speak softly and carry a big stick." Thus Theodore Roosevelt summarized his political wisdom. Indeed, the arguments of pain and fear are persuasive. Whips, chains, prisons, torture, brutality, military power, economic sanctions—all these forms of violence have been extensively used to assert power. From your own life as a child or from your dealings with your own children you know that pain and fear are often rather effective.

But experience has taught us that when we sow the wind, we are likely to reap storms. If brute force, in the short run, succeeds in controlling the weak most of the time, in the long run its results are incalculable. Violence breeds resentment and hatred, and these are the seeds of rebellion. Even torturers know that their techniques have definite limitations. Frantz Fanon tells of a professional torturer who reported, as he underwent psychiatric treatment, that in his *metier* "what you must not do is to give the chap the impression that he won't get away alive from you. Because then he wonders what's the use of talking if that won't save his life. In that case you'll have no chance at all of getting anything from him."[1] Beyond certain limits, violence ceases to be functional for the purpose of control.

In the long run, control of the imagination is much more effective than the use of violence. The Slave must learn to love his Master. He will then obey willingly. If his values and thoughts can be made to coincide with those of him who dominates, then to obey the Master will be just the same as being free. When this happens we see the act of domination as an expression of mercy. In the last instance, even the purpose of torture must be the conquest of the heart. The body is made to suffer so that the heart will learn to love. "O cruel misunderstanding," thinks Wiston, the man who suffers in the torture chambers of *Nineteen Eighty-Four.* "O stubborn, self-willed exile from the loving breast!" We see two gin-scented tears trickling down the sides of his nose. And then: "But it was all right, everything was all right, the struggle was finished. He had won the victory over himself. He loved Big Brother!"[2]

Anyone who reads Orwell's novel and compares it with *Brave New World* is struck by the fact that violence and repression are

1. Frantz Fanon, *The Wretched of the Earth* (1968), p. 269.
2. George Orwell, *Nineteen Eighty-Four* (1949), p. 300.

rampant in the former, whereas nothing like it happens in the latter. Why? Because in *Nineteen Eighty-Four* imagination has not yet come under the control of Organization. Man still dreams heretical dreams. He is still able to commit "crime-think." In Aldous Huxley's vision, however, the war is over. Man has become totally realistic. His mind is now incapable of going beyond the limits of the dominant reality. His reason is a replica of the operations programed by the Organization. He no longer knows what rebellion is. He is totally functional. His consciousness has suffered a radical transformation, and he identifies being controlled with freedom itself. "Slavery is freedom." Accompanying a recent long article on Skinner in *Time* magazine was a suggestive cartoon which conveys exactly what I am trying to say. One mouse says to the other, "Boy, have I got this guy conditioned! Every time I press the bar down, he drops a piece of food."[3]

Power does not know how to achieve such a result. But science enables it to accomplish this dream. This is indeed the hidden *function* of futurology, of a future "intelligently planned." I do not say that this is a conscious intention. It is not my purpose to accuse futurologists of bad faith. But to the extent that science in our civilization is a function of the economic and military powers, it has no alternative. As it was commissioned to organize space, so it carries the thrust of rationalization to its final consequences: it organizes the future. For the future also is to become a function of present conditions of power. As Paul Goodman has aptly remarked, "Future thinking is, in principle, the extrapolation of our present ways."[4] When we are assured that tomorrow, in the natural order of events, will be better than today, we can enjoy ourselves in peace.

3. "Skinner's Utopia: Panacea, or Path to Hell?" *Time*, September 20, 1971, p. 50.
4. *Utopian Essays and Practical Proposals* (1962), p. 4.

Progress, paradoxically, can be used to justify conservatism."[5]

Futurology is prospective pragmatism. Its basic assumption is that the shape of the world to come is a result of present tendencies. Starting from the dominant conditions of power, it projects a future in which they are preserved and enhanced, while at the same time the dysfunctional elements which now resist it are eliminated. And this implies, besides organization of power on a material basis, the conquest of imagination—so that man will love the future to which he is destined.

Suppose that you find yourself locked inside a room with no windows or doors. No matter how nice the room is, you will very soon experience a boredom which turns into the panic of claustrophobia. There is no way out. Inevitably after a while, you will begin to plan your escape. You will start probing the walls and looking for tools with which to break your way to liberty.

Now imagine that you find yourself in a castle with 1001 luxurious rooms filled with surprises, pleasures, and unexpected experiences. As you get tired of one room you move to the next. And so on, indefinitely. So absorbed will you be that you will not notice that the castle, just like that other single room, has neither doors nor windows. You are equally a prisoner, but you will grow old without ever realizing your own condition, and will assume all along that you are free. Thus you will never look for a way out, and your imagination will be kept in thrall to the expectation of what the next room has in store for you.

This is the first principle for control of the imagination: create so many objects of desire that the mind will be kept moving from one to another, without ever being able to move beyond them.

Anyone sensitive enough to perceive what is taking place in

5. Albert Camus, *The Rebel* (1964), p. 194.

our society knows that this process is already in full operation. Imagination cannot compete with the marvels that are offered to it every day. New cars, new toys, new dresses, new beauty products, and a fantastic procession of gadgets which run from cordless back-scratchers to electric devices for producing orgasm. Too often, imagination no longer has either the power or the time to pursue its own aspirations. Our system of production fills all its horizons with ready-made products, and the only initiative left is to choose and to buy.

According to Toffler, this process will reach undreamed-of proportions in the new superindustrial society toward which we are marching. The possibilities of choice, already enormous, will be gigantic in range. Boredom will be impossible. Everything will change so fast that man will have to constantly be on the move to new options.

Here is the fundamental difference between the past and the future: the pace of having. Traditional societies have been based on permanence. But "the new, fast-forming society is based on transience."[6] Every item will be carefully planned so as to wear out or become rapidly outmoded. Planned obsolescence will dominate all sectors of human life. The stability of objects will be dissolved: they will vanish, right in our hands, as pleasure-delivering entities. And man will have to look for new ones. Toffler illustrates this by citing what Mattel did with the Barbie doll. It announced that a new, improved, prettier doll could be obtained by trading in the old one. "What Mattel did not announce," he remarks, "was that by trading in her old doll for a technologically improved model, the little girl of today, citizen of tomorrow's super industrial world, would learn a fundamental lesson about the new society: that man's relationships with things are increasingly temporary."[7] This sounds like a

6. Alvin Toffler, *Future Shock* (1970), p. 48.
7. *Ibid.*, p. 47.

veritable "conversion" within our social organization: man loses his attachment to material things by learning that they have no lasting substance. The truth of the matter, however, is quite different. Economics is not concerned with the spiritualization of man's life. Things will have to disappear rapidly and the pace of acquisition become much faster because factories must be kept busy. *The transience of things is a means toward the permanence of the economic system.*[8] As Toffler himself acknowledges, in the society of the future we will find ways "to lend whole structures greater permanence at the cost of making their substructures less permanent." This is what he calls "modularism." The secret of a healthy economy is whether the system is able to produce and people are able to buy; the more rapid pace of acquisition derives from a stroke of magic which makes what produced pleasure yesterday incapable of producing it today.

Time, in the new world, will be determined by the rhythm of the "healthy economy," even if that implies creating a permanent restlessness in which man comes to learn that what delights him today yields only boredom or frustration tomorrow. It was disturbing to see, in *Brave New World*, how children were "educated for reality." But it is really frightening that already today Mattel and all the powers that define our own reality are actively engaged in teaching our children the basic rules of the game on which their expansion and permanence depend. Objects will become transient in order to eliminate transience from the structures of domination. The faster pace of having will give stability to their control.

"The packaged experiences offered in the future will reach far beyond the imagination of the average consumer, filling the environment with endless novelties," Toffler adds.[9] This is pre-

8. *Ibid.*, p. 54.
9. *Ibid.*, p. 205.

cisely the point. Fascinated by the innumerable rooms of the castle, who will be able to see that we are locked inside? "Scientific" imagination will make the average man's imagination superfluous. It will become atrophied. Yet he will live in the illusion that he is free. "The people of both the past and the present are still locked into relatively choiceless life ways. The people of the future, whose number increases daily, face not choice but overchoice. For them comes an explosive extension of freedom."[10] The mice inside the Skinner box, instead of having only two levers to chose from, will have thousands. Freedom is defined in supermarket terms, the good supermarket being the one with the widest variety of items. In fact, a new version of the supermarket is what the new superindustrial society most resembles. A rather shocking prospect, indeed. Creative freedom will become impossible. I suspect that the new society is the *Brave New World* under another name. "Ending is better than mending. The more stitches, the less riches,"[11] the voice repeated endlessly in the ears of the children in their sleep, in Huxley's nightmare. And so Mattel rehearses our own children in the principle of transience. The logic of the economy plans its endless expansion, and while it does, imagination is funnelled into proper channels so that men will behave in a functional way.

H. J. Campbell relates a fascinating experiment that he is carrying on with animals.

Every morning at the Institute of Psychiatry in London my rabbits excitedly push their head forward as I fit small plugs to them. The plugs come in contact with thin platinum wires that sit permanently in their brains. When I let go, the animals rush to a lever and start pressing it down with their noses, some 500 times in 15 minutes. Each time they press the lever a minuscule amount of electricity flows to the platinum

10. *Ibid.*, p. 226.
11. Aldous Huxley, *Brave New World* (1946), p. 58.

wires and causes activity in the brain cells there. The wires are in the so-called pleasure areas and the rabbits press the lever because the electricity gives them pleasure.[12]

Levers are pressed because they deliver pleasure. Pressing the lever has become, for the rabbit, the mode of appropriating or relating to pleasure. Suppose a system were to succeed in assuming a monopoly over pleasure, and that the only way for the individual to get it was to press the right lever. That system would arrive at the highest possible degree of control of human behavior. Indeed, much greater than that achieved by the monopoly of means of violence, since it produces the same results without creating the dysfunctional by-products and reactions of the latter. *The rationalization of control thus requires that the monopoly of violence be superseded by the monopoly of pleasure.*

According to Toffler, our traditional economy has some basically dysfunctional elements which could eventually destroy it. Sheer accumulation of capital provokes painful sensations in those who are deprived of it. This was the fundamental reason why Marx predicted the downfall of capitalism. The proletariat suffered, and any class which is systematically forced to endure pain will finally rebel against the order that produces it. But even more, capitalists themselves cannot avoid building up dangerous self-destructive impulses on the unconscious level of their personalities, as a result of the ascetic style of life they have to develop to achieve their goal because asceticism implies the repression of the body, and this runs counter to life itself. Our traditional economy, therefore, has often produced unintended dysfunctional tendencies which may ultimately bring it low.

If the system really internalizes the lesson of the rabbits it will proceed to establish a monopoly of pleasure, and man will learn

12. H. J. Campbell, "The Ultimate Pleasure," 1971.

that he can always have pleasure if he is rightly related to it.

Our traditional economy ignored this fact. It was too materialistic and stupid. One knew very well that a variety of commodities gave pleasure, but also that they were not the only source of it. There is a wide range of psychic, religious, mystical, aesthetic, and bodily experiences which are extremely rewarding and which are not commodities. They are free. But this situation is quite dangerous. So long as it exists, the system has not yet established a total monopoly over the sources of pleasure. Man is still able to imagine the possibility of finding satisfaction without pressing a lever. Moreover, the free areas of pleasure beyond institutional control may eventually give rise to the notion that other forms of social organization are possible. And this is ultimately dysfunctional—subversive. It conspires against the closed rationality of the system.

This is the second principle of the control of imagination: there must be no free pleasure. If the system wants to retain the monopoly of power, it must find means to establish a monopoly of pleasure. The ultimate organization of control demands that science find ways of reducing all forms of pleasure to a mode of appropriation functional to the system. Pleasure must be transformed into a commodity—only things that can be bought should be able to produce it. This is the secret of the "elegant scientific revolution" which is the foundation of the "Brave New World."

Books and loud noises, flowers and electric shocks—already in the infant mind these couples were compromisingly linked; and after two hundred repetitions of the same or a similar lesson would be wedded indissolubly. What man has joined, nature is powerless to put asunder.

They'll grow up with what the psychologists used to call an "instinctive" hatred of books and flowers. Reflexes unalterably conditioned. They'll be safe from books and botany all their lives. . . .

If the children were made to scream at the sight of a rose that was on grounds of high economic policy. Not so very long ago . . . they were conditioned to like flowers—flowers in particular and wild nature in general. The idea was to make them want to be going out into the country at every available opportunity, and so compel them to consume transport. . . . But primroses and landscapes have one great defect: they are gratuitous. A love of nature keeps no factories busy. It was decided to abolish the love of nature . . . but *not* the tendency to consume transport. For, of course, it was essential that they should keep going to the country, even though they hated it. The problem was to find an economically sounder reason for consuming transport than a mere affection for primroses and landscapes. It was duly found.

We condition the masses to hate the country . . . but simultaneously we condition them to love all country sports. At the same time, we see to it that all country sports shall entail the use of elaborate apparatus. So that they consume manufactured articles as well as transport.[13]

This is the future toward which we march. We are already "witnessing the beginning of the final break up of industrialism and, with it, the collapse of technocratic planning," proclaims Toffler. "In both its capitalist and communist variants, industrialism was a system focussed on the maximization of material welfare. Technocratic planning is econocentric." But now we move to another economy in which the whole field of psychic, emotional, and human experience—those areas where pleasure is still free—will be transformed into commodities. "The essence of tomorrow's economy," he says, "will be an emphasis upon the *inner* as well as the material needs of individuals and groups. We shall go far beyond any 'functional' necessity, turning the service, whether it is shopping, dining or having one's hair cut, into a *pre-fabricated experience*. As we advance into the future, more and more experiences will be sold strictly on their own merits, *exactly as if they were things*."[14]

The rabbit gets its kicks by pressing the lever; we get ours by

13. Huxley, *op. cit.*, pp. 23–25.
14. Toffler, *op. cit.*, pp. 396–97.

buying. Emotional experiences become goods. They are sold like bubble gum and dog food—"as if they were things." The spiritualization of economy is nothing more than the final reduction of the spirit to the condition of canned food. Within the superindustrial society there is only one means of appropriation left: that of buying. "*All* physical and intellectual senses are replaced by the simple alienation of *all* these senses; the sense of *having.*"[15] These were prophetic words uttered more than a century ago. Even your hatred of the superindustrial society becomes a commodity which helps the economy grow. Are you unhappy, full of anger? Do you want to destroy? "We will have enclaves of the past—communities in which the turnover, novelty and choice are deliberately limited. Such communities not only should not be derided, they should be subsidized by the larger society as a form of mental and social insurance. "[16] This is an area which promises fantastic possibilities of investment. If you can, you will pay the cost of your stay. What about spending a summer in one of these enclaves of the past? They will offer the thrill and excitement one gets today from a safari in Africa. If you cannot, never mind. Enjoy your rebellion. It is free. Society pays for it, you know; it is part of the "social insurance" taxes. For the system it is better to have you satisfied than making trouble. By the way: is not this strangely similar to the Savage Reservation of *Brave New World?*

But behind its most exciting promises futurology tells something, almost in a whisper, that makes us shudder: *there is no way out.* The future is inevitable. It is useless to look for alternatives, and all plans of escape are doomed to failure. The future lies ahead of me, like this wall in my office.

15. Karl Marx, "Private Property and Labor," in Erich Fromm, *Marx's Concept of Man* (1964), p. 132.
16. Toffler, *op. cit.,* p. 346.

We shall *collide* with it, just as I will collide with the wall if I walk toward it. The future is *arriving*, as winter is arriving.[17]

The future becomes a thing, an alien thing in relation to which I am totally impotent. Whether I like it or not, whether I aspire to it or not, whether I hope for it or not, it will come. All one can do is to accept its inevitability and be ready for the "unavoidable adaptative experience."

Obviously, the future is not a direct product of man's intention. The very assumption of Toffler and others that it will produce shock is a symptom of how little it is now the result of "conscious human guidance." If the future had grown out of me, as my child, as the creation of my desires, how could it be shocking? I would receive it with joy. It would be the fulfillment of my hopes.

Future shock is a symptom. It shows that history is not being made by man. The powers that hold monopolies of violence and of pleasure in the world are exactly those that now claim a monopoly over the future. If the future is likely to produce imbalance or insanity in man, the reason is not to be found in his inability to face change, but rather in his refusal to accept the kinds of change that result from the insanity of power.

When imagination is convinced of the inevitability of the future, it learns its own helplessness at the same time. Like mice in a box, men see that there is no way out. The game has to be played with the levers provided. Imagination becomes a useless function. Man is free "to be atheist or Jew, heterosexual or homosexual, John Bircher or Communist."[18] Why? Has he become really freer? No. He can be whatever he likes, since his imagination makes no difference at all. Once he is castrated and transformed into a eunuch, he may be allowed to enter and live

17. *Ibid.*, pp. 11, 13, 371.
18. *Ibid.*, p. 89.

in the harem. The only way to avoid the pain that comes from knowing the futility of one's dreams and the uselessness of one's hatred of the shocking future is to forget dreams and become adapted to the inevitable.

" 'Stability,' insisted the Controller, 'stability. The primal and ultimate need. Stability.' "[19] These words come to us from Huxley's vision. "Modularism," proclaim our futurologists. "Change everything, move everything around, create infinite varieties of choices." But beyond the reach of man's hand and invisible to his eye, the structures of power remain, omnipotent.

The future is shocking, not because of its novelty but because it will make novelty impossible. As Henri Lefebvre suggests,

With the advent of the kingdom of pure technology we will no longer have a historical future and we will no longer know temporality as we now do. The past will be reduced to memory—in its cybernetical sense: the store of used combinations. It will be a simultaneous past, without a history. The future and the possible will be reduced to the combinations not yet used, always in finite number. The informational and cybernetical future is a future without history. We will enter in a sort of everlasting present . . . of the machines, combinations, arrangements and permutations of the given elements. The only new happenings will be the introductions of new techniques.[20]

Just as happened with the pragmatists, one assumes that there is nothing wrong with the whole. We refuse to ask the *Why?* question—the question that forces us to consider the foundation upon which the future is being built—and move ahead triumphantly with the results of the *How?* question. And as we move deep into the future, we plunge deeper still into the quagmire of the irrational presuppositions of the structures of power that control our present. And because our imagination

19. Huxley, *op. cit.,* p. 49.
20. Henri Lefebvre, "Reflexões sôbre o Estruturalismo e a História" (1967), pp. 82, 89. My translation.

has been castrated, we are unable to see alternatives. We are convinced that there is no way out. As a consequence, we are incapable of a creative act—the only thing that could free us from the logic of the dinosaur and open the way to a genuinely new future.

3

The Ideology of the Absurd: Realism

"Lieutenant Calley never used the word 'kill,' " said the psychiatrist who examined him in the wake of the My Lai massacre. The lieutenant told him that the military avoided that word because it caused "very negative emotional reactions" among the men, who had been taught the commandment "Thou shall not kill."[1]

Out of the very depth of their being and of the childhood memories that constituted the emotional matrix of their lives, the GIs *knew* that it was not right to kill a person. This was not a mere abstract principle. Killing implied not only the death of a human being, but an act of violence against values which were at the foundation of their own personalities. Hence the unavoidable need to resist. If they did not go as far as open acts of military insubordination, their resistance was nevertheless there, within themselves, in the form of a disturbed conscience.

But the logic of power demanded that triggers be pulled. It has no room for humanistic concerns and for the reasons of the

1. *New York Times,* February 23, 1971, p. 12.

heart. And how shall one solve this problem? How see that the killing goes on, without inner resistance, without "negative emotional reactions," without a guilty conscience? How transform a painful experience into a pleasant or at least endurable one? How totally adjust the consciousness of men to the logic of power?

The solution is simple. The word *killing* is charged with emotional elements. So one must no longer associate pulling a trigger with the act of killing. Another word is used: *waste.* Triggers are pulled. The enemy is effectively killed. The military logic achieves its goal and consciences are not disturbed. The act no longer produces pain; it is neutral, and can eventually give satisfaction or even pleasure. The miracle has been accomplished by a simple change of words.

This is a very important aspect of the human experience. We are unable to confront reality immediately. We cannot actually see it, as it were, face to face. Things come to us not in their naked factualness but clothed in language. The words attached to them partly determine how we experience the world around us. And because of their power to define our world, they ultimately condition what we do. As Robert Merton has pointed out, "Our conceptual language tends to fix our perceptions and, derivatively, our thought and behavior. The concept defines the situation."[2] Hence the importance of language in the control of imagination and therefore as a means of political control. Language tends to define what is possible and what is not, what gives pleasure and what does not. By contrast to what happens with animals, our feelings of pain and pleasure are conditioned by the words attached to the relevant experience.

Sex is supposed to produce pleasure. But if one attaches the word *sin* to it, one cannot avoid the painful sense of guilt that

2. Robert K. Merton, *On Theoretical Sociology* (1967), p. 145.

follows. I remember the struggle of a young Jewish student, torn between the physical stimuli that reached his nose from a Brazilian *feijoada* (a dish in which black beans and pork find an almost metaphysical harmony), and his concepts of kosher and nonkosher food. Women especially have become acutely aware of how language defines the world. A number of times I have been interrupted in classes or conversations because of my use of the word *man* to cover mankind in general (but even *man-kind* is biased, being *man*kind). Very often I get impatient, but the fact is that they are right to the extent that our use of words defines a world dominated by men. Every word has a world around itself. As Wittgenstein put it, "The limits of my language mean the limits of my world."[3]

The human world is thus radically different from the world of nature, in that nature is there whether I want it or not, whereas the human world comes into being through the media-tion of our will. To the extent that it is conditioned by language, it is the result of the meanings *we create*. Whites gave a bad meaning to the word *black*. Blacks are rejecting it and recreat-ing their world around the idea that "black is beautiful." The concept was created that sex is sin—and it was actually lived as sin until other people were able to speak of it without shame and even with joy. I learned, from an imported Protestant church where I found myself, that my Latin-American culture was ugly and to be despised, that the true values of life were the American ones (i.e., those of the United States). It took me a long time to learn to dance and enjoy the samba, because the only thing I knew was how to sing American gospel songs.

The human world does not have for us the factualness of nature. It depends on intention and will. Even the way I experi-ence nature is ultimately determined by the language I use to

3. Ludwig Wittgenstein, *Tractatus Logico-Philosophicus* (1961), p. 115.

refer to it. Death is a fact of nature. But the way I live my life, i.e., this period of time between my being alive right now and my future physical death, is not a fact of nature. Indeed, I have never experienced death. My experience of it will be the end of all experience. My way of living death right now is determined by the words and symbols I use when I *name* this natural fact. Social reality, as Berger and Luckmann have shown, is a reality of a different kind. It is a product of will, a result of what men have done, do, and will do. It is a social construct. Language has no autonomous existence. It is part of the social reality and comes into being when we speak. "A word hasn't got a meaning given to it, as it were, by a power independent of us. A word has the meaning someone has given to it."[4]

When I speak, regardless of how objective I want to be, it is out of my own self-understanding that I speak. My existential situation, my values, my autobiography as I have written it in the words of my mind: this is the origin of my language. Besides defining the limits of my world, language reveals the limits of my self.

This is the basic assumption behind the projective tests in psychology. Even if I speak about a thing, about a picture, about an inkblot—the way I speak, the way I put things together, and the way I organize that world is governed by that same autobiography. Here I am assuming, obviously, that there is no human being who has not written his story in one way or another. If there were such a one, he would not be an actual person, for our consciousness is a product of our life story. Indeed, consciousness is the plot of that story. It is a *way* of organizing our memories. When we look back we discover that our past is not an undifferentiated succession of events, one after the other. There are zones of clarity and darkness, of pride and shame, of

4. Ludwig Wittgenstein, *The Blue and Brown Books* (1958), p. 28.

pleasure and pain. Some rooms are carefully locked, and we hope they will never be opened again. Others are filled with experiences we hold precious, which give us joy. This is the basis upon which psychoanalytical theory is built. It takes language as the way to one's being—but a being who is a drama, story with a plot, with villains and heroes, with times of pleasure and times of pain. Under everything the patient says about the world is the unconscious plot, trying to make the world support its own solution for the life problem. The individual, remarked Lecky, is "a unified system with two sets of problems—one the problem of maintaining inner harmony within himself [the plot must be preserved], and the other the problem of maintaining harmony with the environment, especially the social environment, in the midst of which he lives."[5]

Our behavior depends on how our autobiography is related to the world around us—our plot to the reading of newspapers, our story to history, our emotions, values, and expectations to what Organization is producing. When my plot is confirmed by my reading of the reality around me—or more precisely, when I succeed in organizing the information I take in so as to harmonize with my autobiography—I have the good feeling of being at home. The world confirms my version of what is taking place, and I tend to be adjusted to it. This is what took place in this country before the sixties. Biography and history, self-identity and national ideology, individual and Organization were harmoniously blended.

But if, on the contrary, I cannot harmonize the world that surrounds me with my plot; if I feel that reality does not confirm my expectations as to what should be taking place—then I experience discomfort and finally pain. I no longer feel at home, and my behavior becomes dysfunctional. I resist being transformed

5. Prescott Lecky, *Self-Consistency: A Theory of Personality* (1961), p. 111.

into a function, because I feel that Organization runs counter to my values. I reject the proposed future. My vision of it is shocking because I sense that it will not be the fulfillment of my expectations. It does not grow out of my self. It is an alien phenomenon, forced upon me, which causes "very negative emotional reactions," just as the act of killing did among GIs.

Whenever man takes his emotions, values, and aspirations seriously, he will sooner or later be forced to resist the natural course of events. In short: the logic of the heart tends to breed discontent, resistance, and ultimately rebellion. And the need for rationalization of power and the functional requirements of Organization cannot tolerate this. They have to find ways, not only of reducing imagination to impotence, but of convincing man that this is for his own good. In other words, man must internalize the ideology of Organization, so that as he tells his own story he will dismiss the plot that grew out of his desires and imagination and accept what he is told by Organization as the true version of life. *He must accept adaptation and conformity as the paradigms of normality and sanity.* And conversely, he must accept desire and imagination as symptoms of sickness or unbalance and error.

Conceive of a person who is going through a situation of great suffering. His body and heart tell him that this should not be so. Every groan is a protest. Every tear is an indictment of the dominant order of things. Unconsciously he is repeating to himself: "What is, cannot be true." Suppose however that he is taught, and finally believes, that this is the will of God. This transformation has a remarkable consequence. If his suffering is the will of God, man "learns" that his protests are useless. His desires have no connection with reality, which is quite independent of his wishes. And the only thing he can do is to accept it with stoic resignation. He must adapt himself. The dysfunctional and dangerously disturbing possibilities of his experience

are dissolved by means of a religious metaphysics which in-
structs him in the futility of his own feeling, the uselessness of
his desires, the madness of his imagination, and the irreducible
ultimacy of the reality that surrounds him.

Here is the secret: for man's behavior to be "rationalized," he
must be convinced of the irrelevance of the logic of the heart
and the inevitability of the logic of "reality." He must become
objective. He is to be convinced that his imagination weaves
illusions. He must abdicate his will and bow down to the "reality" of life. He must be converted to "realism." This is the
ideology of our civilization. What used to be accomplished by
means of a religious metaphysical language is now achieved by
the philosophical, scientific, and psychoanalytical developments which have become the canonical language of our era.

The "official" version of our biographies was first elaborated
by the Enlightenment. This word in itself is quite revealing. It
contains, in condensed form, a global vision of the epic of man
—a new self-understanding of what it means to be human. Into
this global world view our biographies are made to fit, as parts
of a gigantic jigsaw puzzle.

Where does man come from? The Enlightenment looked
back, and what did it see? Man, submerged in darkness, dominated by the irrational, under the power of instinctual forces
which kept him blind and captive. Little by little, however, he
rises from that level. Scales fall from his eyes. He sees. Demons
are expelled. And he finally becomes lord of himself and of his
destiny. The night is past. Day dawns. It is the era of light, the
Age of Reason.

There may be variations in telling the story, but the theme
is the same. In Comte's famous phenomenology of the human
spirit, man moves out of his emotional, instinctual, religious
childhood, through metaphysics, toward—finally—maturity:
positive thinking. Man has come of age. It is the victory of pure

reason over desire, of objective thought over imagination, of the logic of reality over the logic of the heart.

Human life takes place in the context of an objective reality over which man has no power. Before any experience of the world, before the heart began to love, reality was already there. What is left for man is to *discover* it, provided that he frees himself from the illusory interference of his emotions. This is true not only of the physical universe but of the ethical sphere also. This is what Kant's two *Critiques* want to prove. As man can know the structure of nature, he can also know the structure of the good. It is interesting to observe how behind Kant's rather abstract philosophical investigations one always finds a deep political concern, exactly the same as that expressed in the French Revolution: the hope of establishing an order which will no longer be the result of expediency, force, and passion, but the simple embodiment of reason. If reason reveals to man what the nature of the good is, then it is possible to build a universal society based on truth and justice.

It is not difficult to see why emotions cannot have any role to play in this world view. They are the archenemy of pure reason. "Passions," says Kant, "are cancers for pure practical reason. . . . It is folly . . . that strictly contradicts reason even in its formal principle. . . . Passions are not only . . . *unfortunate* moods that are pregnant with many evils, but also, without exception, wicked. . . . [They are] not only *pragmatically* pernicious but also *morally* reprehensible."[6]

Emotions, like desires and imagination, grow out of the particularity of our situation. If one acts out this emotional matrix, one is bound to go against the universal truth. Wherever emotion is, neither truth nor goodness is to be found, according to

6. Immanuel Kant, *Anthropologie* (1798), § 71. Quoted by Walter Kaufmann in *Hegel: A Reinterpretation* (1965), pp. 34–35. For the sake of simplicity I have omitted a number of qualifying and explanatory parentheses in the text.

Kant. This is why he insisted that the grounds of action must be totally free from such interference. An act which is performed "out of love," even if it coincides with the requirements of duty, is a priori wrong.

The foregoing are the directives by which our biographies and autobiographies are still to be written. Here we learn which are the zones of darkness and shame, and which are pages of light and pride. Our personal unconscious is ultimately under the power of the collective unconscious of our civilization. This is the origin of our repression.

So if our civilization were to create a myth of the origins of man, it would run something like this: Once upon a time there was an ape which was different from all the others, because he had a serious trouble with his eyes. In the evolutionary process something went wrong and his eyes were, by an unfortunate mistake, connected with his heart. The horrible result was that, instead of seeing things as they really were, as other animals did, this ape mixed them up with his desires. He was surrounded by an inhospitable desert, but he did not see it as such. His heart made him see it as the land of his dreams: green meadows, creeks with fresh water, trees, fruits, and peace. Obviously this was nothing more than an illusion. But he could not resist it. Over and over again he left his safe place and walked toward it, as if it were true. The results were always tragic. Reality does not correspond to our expectations. He found nothing but stones, burning sands, and cactus. Each time he almost died of hunger and thirst. He managed to find his way home, but his body was covered with blisters, thorns, and bruises.

This happened again and again, until one day he said to himself, "I cannot trust either my eyes or my heart, and I know that I cannot resist the vision. My instinctive drive to go after it is irresistible. Yet every time I yield to the temptation my life is endangered and my desires are frustrated. I need something to protect myself." So he built a high circular wall—so high that he could not climb it—around himself. From that time on, he continued to be disturbed by his heart and to have visions of a world created by desire—but every time it happened, he knocked his head against the wall and was brought back to reality. This is how man was born. And this is why he built civilization. It is repressive—true. But not by accident. Its function is to be repressive, because otherwise he will die.

We can easily imagine Freud in his later years thus recounting the story of man. His clinical discovery of the function of the pleasure principle in drawing up the program of man's life by no means converted him from his personal commitment to the ideology of the Enlightenment. On the contrary, he only became the more convinced of the essential insanity of our desires and of the need to repress the logic of the heart. The primitive with his magic, the child with its play, and the neurotic with his illusions think and behave under the impulse of a common psychic dynamic: "the excessive valuation of their wishes."[7] If we look back to the origins of our present, the Freudian mythology points to these three symbols. They are expressions of a phase which has already been overcome. As maturity succeeds childhood, normality is to conquer neurosis and science is to displace magic. "In the beginning was Desire"—thus starts the myth. But it ends by affirming, "And it will be no more." Magic, play, and neurosis, as affirmations of the pleasure principle, are zones of shadow and shame. Light and pride, on the contrary, are found when man moves beyond the pleasure principle. The "primacy of the intellect" will finally overcome the irrationality of the heart, and the gods of men will be displaced by the new god, the *Logos* of scientific reason.[8] History is man educating

7. Sigmund Freud, *Totem and Taboo* (1946), p. 110.
8. Sigmund Freud, *The Future of an Illusion* (1964), p. 88.

himself for reality. He achieves maturity, he finds sanity. He becomes a realist.

Marxism is a different version of the same premises. It, too, is a product of the Enlightenment and twin brother to psychoanalytical theory, although it prefers to ignore the fact.

"Why is man deceived?" it asks. "What is the reason why his consciousness becomes 'false consciousness,' thereby falsifying his whole understanding of reality?" The answer: being caught up emotionally in the material interests which belong to his concrete economic situation, man is misled by his heart. The consequence is that he cannot see with the objectivity which pertains to scientific knowledge, becoming, as a consequence, a prey of ideological distortions.[9]

Marx's critique of ideology is a weapon he uses against the left-wing Hegelians. These philosophers believed that consciousness was the basis of reality, and that one could revolutionize reality by revolutionizing consciousness. Marx's battle against them is identical with Freud's attack on magic: one cannot change the world by the nature of thought.

So far, so good. But the Marxists go a step further. From the discovery that imagination may be a form of illusion, they come to the conclusion that imagination *is* illusion. Proceeding from this basic axiom, scientific socialism asserts that in order to establish a true science of history the first thing is to *disentangle history from imagination.* "In the history of society," writes Engels, "the mere actors are all endowed with consciousness; they are agents imbued with deliberation and passion, men working towards an appointed end; nothing appears without an intentional purpose, without an end desired." However, if "the ends of the actions are intended, the results which follow from the actions are not intended, or in so far as they appear to

9. These remarks refer specifically to so-called "scientific Marxism" and not to the young Marx.

correspond with the end desired, in their final results are quite different from the conclusion wished."[10] Emotions and intentions are there, but they play no role in the building of history. They are results—not causes. History moves ahead by virtue of its material reality; if man plays a role, it is totally determined by the direction of the structural dynamics of the social reality. Marx could thus affirm that "it is totally irrelevant what this proletarian or even the whole proletariat directly imagines. What matters is *what is* and what one will have to do historically because of this reality."[11] Imagination must be abolished, for two reasons. First, it is the source of false consciousness. And second, it is not one of the forces behind the historical dynamic. It is not an object of the science of history.

If imagination does not create history, a basic question remains to be answered: "What driving forces stand in turn behind these motives of action? What are the historical causes which transform themselves into motives of action in the brains of the agents?"[12] The essence of the Marxist science becomes clear. It consists in "the knowledge of the independence of the forces which actually move history vis-à-vis the psychic consciousness that men might have of them.[13]

It is the same story. Marxism remains rigorously with the script proposed by the Enlightenment. Where Kant saw in history a movement from emotions to pure reason; where Freud described it as an evolution from instinct to intellect; and where Comte considered it a progressive development from religious to positive thinking—Marxism sees a revolution which abandons *ideology* and discovers *science*. There is an objective his-

10. Friedrich Engels, *Feuerbach: The Roots of the Socialist Philosophy* (1912), pp. 104–105.
11. Quoted by Georg Lukács, *Historia y Consciencia de Clase* (1969), p. 49. My translation.
12. Engels, *op cit.*, p. 106.
13. Lukács, *op. cit.*, p. 50.

torical truth. It is there, to be found. The question is not to
create new ideals. History is not made by preaching. Ideals are
for Marx what values are for Freud: figments of the imagination.
This is why Marxism has been so ruthlessly opposed to the
utopian socialists, who believed that reason can be creative, that
the human will can transcend the limits of the dominant structures, and that behavior is not a simple by-product of social
reality. They trusted that something new could be created
which was not simply the result of present social contradictions.
The utopian had confidence in the power of the spirit and in the
possibility of freedom as over against the determinism of
material forces. He assumed that man is actually the creator of
history.

Not so Marx, who strongly rejected any suggestion that he
was a preacher of social reform or a prophet of a new utopia.
"Communism," he declared, "is for us not a state which is to be
established, an *ideal* to which reality will have to adjust itself.
We call communism the *real* movement which abolishes the
present state of things."[14]

Scientific socialism is a form of realism. The possibility of the
science of history depends on the assumption that history is an
object of knowledge in the same sense as objects studied by the
physical sciences. It is assumed to be a structure and a process
which can be known by means of observation and quantification. "My analytical method," Marx affirms, "does not start from
man but from the economically given social period."[15] History
is a structure complete in itself, ultimately determined by the
quantitative elements of economics. Where is man? He is absent from the field of theoretical explanation. As Althusser put
it, "one can and must speak openly of Marx's *theoretical anti-
humanism*, and see in this *theoretical anti-humanism* the abso-

14. Karl Marx and Friedrich Engels, *The German Ideology* (1947), p. 26.
15. Quoted by Louis Althusser, *For Marx* (1970), p. 219.

lute (negative) precondition of the (positive) knowledge of the human world itself, and of its practical transformation."[16]

History assumes the status of a physical object, as does the future it is engendering. Who can guarantee that the future will not be just as shocking as the one announced by Toffler? Marxism becomes science, thanks to the reification of history. According to the program drawn up by the Enlightenment, it is not the function of reason to be creative. As sanity, for Freud, implied man's submission and adaptation to the reality principle, so in scientific Marxism historical truth demands that consciousness become a mirror of reality. As Engels put it, "Modern socialism is nothing but the reflex, in thought, of this conflict in fact."[17] Realism explains *how* history happens. Its material consists of structural forces: these are the factors responsible for what is today and for what will be in the future. Subjectivity, therefore, must be nothing more than a faithful reflection of what objectively takes place. There is no room for imagination left. By learning *how* history happens, one learns *why* imagination must be eliminated. And man thus accepts the need of his own repression. "It is the will of God!" "It is the will of reality!"

And how has the non-Communist part of the Western world described the epic of man? What broad premises has it provided for our own evaluation of our personal stories? The answer to these questions is not as easy as when we analyze Marxism, since we lack a collection of authoritative texts. Our notion of history is more complex. For us, it results from the intermingling of a number of different factors, most of them unconscious.

Where shall we start? As we all know from psychoanalysis, most of the time we are not aware of the forces that control our lives. We live out our everyday routines ignoring the fact that

16. *Ibid.*, p. 229.
17. Friedrich Engels, *Socialism: Utopian and Scientific* (n.d.), p. 97.

our ways of thinking and acting depend on an unconscious plot which structures our own being. But though we are not aware of our unconscious, this does not mean it does not exist, but simply that its ways of controlling us are more insidious and pervasive. Since we do not see it we have no way of criticizing it. We are under its power.

The same is true of communities, countries, and even civilizations. There is something that could be called the "collective unconscious"—that tacit script or set of unspoken directives which governs the ways we experience life. As Althusser points out, our ideologies in most cases have little to do with "consciousness." "They are usually images and occasionally concepts, but it is above all as *structures* that they impose on the vast majority of men, not via their consciousness."[18]

How do we get to the unconscious? By looking at the *style of behavior* it produces. The *style of our behavior* reflects, as in a mirror, the *structure of our unconscious*.

And what is our style? We are pragmatists.

Pragmatism is a way of asking questions: "How can I do this? How can I solve this concrete problem?"[19] Its concern with practical issues gives one the impression that here at last we find an attitude free of ideological and metaphysical distortions. Indeed, pragmatism is sure that reality does not consist of either emotions or ideas. Reality is a number of quantifiable, concrete problems which can be attacked with the help of scientific, value-free procedures. A few years ago it became common to speak of "the end of ideology." Nothing could be more to the taste of pragmatism, which believes that our emotions—our desires and volitional prejudices—are what make the solution of the real problems of life impossible. Once we forget these disturbing factors and begin to deal with life problems as with

18. Althusser, *op. cit.*, p. 233.
19. Karl Mannheim, *Ideology and Utopia* (1936), p. 229.

mathematical ones, we have some chance of discovering the key to their solution. The wisdom of science replaces the madness of the heart.

However, things are not so simple. As Lecky once remarked, "All scientific creations are not only symbolic representations of so called external events, but arrangements to serve our human need for self-consistency."[20] Our objective insights are related to emotional roots which are not "rational." Pragmatism is the symptom of a world view. It is the style produced by a way of understanding history and biography—reality—and consequently what it means to be human. What lies behind the pragmatic questions? "In all these questions we sense the optimistic undertone: I need not worry about the whole, the whole will take care of itself."[21]

This is the unconfessed ideology of pragmatism: there is nothing wrong with the system. Pragmatism is the style of operation of the man who feels at home. His biography fits very well in the whole. Psychoanalytically he is sane: he is the adjusted and adapted person. Although he may be quite ignorant of the philosophy of the Enlightenment, he unconsciously believes that the Age of Reason has dawned. Reason has become a social system. This is why he no longer needs to worry about the whole, for the whole is merely the solution of all actual and possible problems. Thus, there is only one problem that pragmatism *cannot* see: the structural one. By definition the whole is eliminated from its consideration as a problem. On the contrary, it provides the logic for the solution of all problems.

So if we ask pragmatism to tell us how it sees history taking place, we will get an answer quite similar to sociological functionalism. Functionalism sees society as if it were an organism. In the organism limbs, organs, and systems, all are functions of

20. Lecky, *op. cit.*, p. 75.
21. Mannheim, *op. cit.*, p. 229.

a greater whole. It is the whole that determines what functions are needed and what operations must be performed. The various parts are no more than means to an ultimate end, which is the preservation of the whole.

According to this logic, no function which is vital to the whole can be eliminated. Take the heart, for instance. This organ is vital for circulation of the blood. If circulation stops, the body dies. You can exchange the heart for a mechanical device which performs the same function, but you cannot eliminate the function itself.

Applied to society, this principle asserts that *the form of a system is the limit of its possibilities*. One may exchange certain items for "functional alternatives," but one cannot do anything that goes against the basic needs of survival of the system. *"Any attempts to eliminate an existing social structure without providing adequate alternative structures for fulfilling the functions previously fulfilled by the abolished organization is doomed to failure,"* says Merton.[22] But since the social system is what determines its own vital functions, one might as well rephrase the statement to say: *The system sees to it that only changes which contribute to its perpetuation shall survive.* For all practical purposes, pragmatism and functionalism identify the social system with reality. This is the secret of realism.

What happens to desire and imagination? They have the same fate as in Marxism. If the system is what ultimately determines the shape and limits of the possible, all the creations of imagination which go beyond these limits are defined a priori as utopian and unrealizable. What moves society is the dynamics of the system and not our intentions. This is why social analysis must be concerned with "the observable objective consequences" and never with "the subjective dispositions."

22. Merton, *op. cit.*, p. 135.

"Whenever it mistakenly identifies (subjective) motives with (objective) funtions, it abandons a lucid functional approach."[23] There is an element of truth in this remark. In a society in which imagination and intention have been reduced to impotence by the organization of power, social analysis actually does not find them among the elements that make history. It is understandable that science should thus describe *what* is happening. However, *to transform this fact into a value* and to promote the factual removal of imagination into the metaphysics of realism is rather unscientific. It would seem that a fateful mistake is being made here in taking a symptom of disease for a sign of health. I can love a dinosaur who sees his condition and cries. But I cannot love a dinosaur who sees his condition and says, "That is how it should be."

Merton makes the ideological assumptions of functionalism still clearer when he says that *"to seek social change, without due recognition of the manifest and latent functions performed by the social organization undergoing change, is to indulge in social ritual rather than social engineering."*[24] Precisely the same argument that Marxism used against the utopians, who assumed that the frontiers of the possible are far broader than the limits of the present and actual. They believed that desire, will, and imagination could move communities so that they would be able to create a future qualitatively different from what is now on hand. But our ideology, like Marxism, says No. Imagination has no role to play in the creation of the future. I must correct myself here: imagination cannot be creative. It cannot create a new *form* of social organization. But it can move things around so as to keep the system going. In functionalism, the ultimacy of the social system corresponds to Toffler's idea of modularism: whole structures remain untouched while

23. *Ibid.*, p. 107.
24. *Ibid.*, p. 135.

internal changes take place. Creative imagination is displaced and modular imagination takes its place.

The religious man overcame his imagination by saying, "It is the will of God." We achieve the same result by saying, "The claims of my imagination are not supported by the facts of reality." Therefore imagination is nonsense. The function of the old theology is taken over by the new religion: realism.

Imagination is not actually eliminated. But by applying to it the labels of insanity and unrealism we learn *why* it must not be taken seriously. You may be "atheist or Jew, heterosexual or homosexual, John Bircher or Communist"—provided you do not allow these elements to meddle with "reality." Imagination is allowed to remain as an idiosyncrasy, devoid of historical significance. You may enjoy it in your bedroom in the form of dreams, in your living room, museum, or concert hall in the form of art, and you may even daydream if you are careful to define this as a secluded area of the mind which does not interfere with the "real" world.

We live in two kingdoms, just as in the old Lutheran doctrine. As a matter of fact, the polarity of grace and freedom versus law of Lutheran theology is exactly the same as the Freudian conflict between the pleasure and reality principles. They are both ideologies for the repression of imagination. If we are convinced that life is to be lived in two separate spheres, this explains to us why it is that reality enjoys an autonomy of its own, whereas my desires must be confined to my inner life. The repression of the logic of the heart is thus explained and accepted. It goes without saying that existential theology and the theology of secularization are to a great degree religious forms of the ideology of realism and thus have provided a religious rationale for the displacement of imagination from the centers of power.

But realism is an illusion. Its great accomplishment is the

magic transubstantiation it performs in calling Organization by the name *reality*. Indeed, its theory and methods assume that Organization has the same ontological status as nature. One analyzes the social order with the same methods used in exploring the physical universe: observation and quantification. There is more wisdom in Humpty Dumpty than in most of our scientists—at least he knows that these two orders are qualitatively different. And the element that makes all the difference is *power*.

"When *I* use a word," Humpty Dumpty said, in a rather scornful tone, "it means just what I choose it to mean—neither more nor less."

"The question is," said Alice, "whether you *can* make words mean so many different things."

"The question is," said Humpty Dumpty, "which is to be the master —that's all."[25]

If we were to take this solemnly, it is clear that Alice is naïve. She believes that words have a meaning in themselves. She is the prototype of the scientist who takes nature as the looking glass through which he sees the political order. The result is inevitable: he is prevented from seeing the realities of power. Of this Humpty Dumpty, in his peremptory way, is aware. The meaning of a word is ultimately dependent on the power of the one who utters it. Teddy Roosevelt knew it was useless merely to "speak softly." Soft speech by itself is impotent to organize power. This is why the big stick is needed. It is the Master who defines the reality of the Slave. The "meanings" of the defeated, if not forgotten, are defined by the victors as falsehood, heresy, and subversion.

Power, as we have seen, creates Organization. This is the political origin and basis of our world.

When a certain language succeeds in *describing* this world

25. Lewis Carroll, *Through the Looking Glass* (1924).

and in *explaining why it has to be so*—when it is able to name it reality and in so doing cover the realities of power that lie behind it—then language becomes power itself. It functions in exactly the same way as Newspeak in *Nineteen Eighty-Four.* "The purpose of Newspeak was not only to provide a medium of expression for the world-view and mental habits proper to the devotees of Ingsoc, but to make all other modes of thought impossible. It was intended that when Newspeak had been adopted once and for all and Oldspeak forgotten, a heretical thought—that is, a thought diverging from the principles of Ingsoc—should be literally unthinkable."[26]

Other modes of thought—a heretical thought—this is what imagination is all about. By setting up the limits of the evident world as the horizon for its language about reality, realism eliminates imagination; declares any attempt to move beyond these limits unscientific, insane, and nonobjective; and thereby performs the function of the *ideology of the powers which succeeds in organizing the world according to their interests.* The philosophy of the Enlightenment, the developments in psychoanalysis, and positivism in science are thus various forms of the ideology of Organization. Science first told power *how* imagination *could* be controlled. And then it tells imagination *why* it *should* be controlled. We become thereby reconciled to the repression of our aspirations and the frustration of our desires. All opposition is dissolved by the magic phrase: "It is the will of reality!" We are first forbidden to go beyond the logic of the dinosaur, and then we discover ourselves not really wanting to go beyond it. Realism is thus the illusion that bewitches us with its proclamation that reality cannot be tampered with, and in so doing, makes man incapable of a creative act.

"Thus, after a long, tortuous, but heroic development, just at

26. George Orwell, *Nineteen Eighty-Four* (1949), p. 303.

the highest stage of awareness, when history is ceasing to be blind fate and is becoming more and more man's own creation," with the abandonment of imagination "man, left without any ideals, becomes a mere creature of impulses."[27] Endowed with the greatest of all possibilities by the wisdom of evolution, man refuses it and prefers to regress to the level of animal behavior. Unable to create, he becomes like the dinosaur. He cannot and does not want to dissolve the irrationality embodied in the very rationalization of his civilization, and is thereby condemned to be destroyed by it.

27. Mannheim, *op. cit.*, p. 236.

Part 2

Imagination
and the Logic of Creativity

All ages prate against each other in your spirits; and the dreams and prating of all ages were yet more real than your waking. You are sterile: that is why you lack faith. But whoever had to create also had his prophetic dreams and astral signs—and faith in faith.

—FRIEDRICH NIETZSCHE

4

Imagination, Creativity, and the Rebirth of Life

Dr. Jay W. Forrester, professor of management at the Massachusetts Institute of Technology, has articulated a new social law which is called Forrester's law. In very simple and crude terms "this maxim holds that in complicated situations efforts to improve things often tend to make them worse, sometimes much worse, on occasion calamitous."[1] Although this sounds like something new, it is not. Indeed, one of the fundamental axioms that control Marxist analysis is that when a system has a built-in contradiction, no matter how hard one tries to remedy this, it will inexorably work itself out toward its ultimate consequences. But these are new and complicated ways of repeating, obscurely, what was said long ago with greater clarity and grace: "No one sews a patch of unshrunk cloth on to an old coat; for then the patch tears away from the coat, and leaves a bigger hole. Neither do you put new wine into old wine-skins; if you do, the skins

1. Harry Schwartz, "Forrester's Law" (1971).

burst, and then the wine runs out and the skins are spoilt" (Matt. 9:16–17).[2]

Dinosaurian pragmatism produces only dinosaurian results. Pragmatism starts with the assumption that there is nothing wrong with the system. Problems are solved by means of modular imagination. Pragmatism is incurably optimistic; it believes that things can be improved indefinitely. Suppose, however, that the system is basically irrational and that its seeming rationality is nothing more than a rationalization of its irrational foundations. Continuing pragmatic procedures and modular imagination will simply perpetuate and aggravate these elements. When a system is irrational, sheer increase in efficacy tends to make its condition worse, much worse—on occasion calamitous.

We live in a sick society.

Norman O. Brown once pointed out that "under the conditions of repression, the repetition-compulsion establishes a fixation to the past, which alienates the neurotic from the present and commits him to the unconscious quest for the past in the future. Thus neurosis exhibits the quest for novelty, but underlying it, at the level of the instincts, is the compulsion to repeat."[3] Is not this the case of our civilization? Everything is organized so that business may go on as usual. The future is to be an extension of our present ways. We are stubbornly committed to finding better ways of doing the same things; indeed, our "better ways" are in fact new ways to perpetuate the old thing! We seem unable to expel the evil spirit of dinosaur logic. And as we pursue our fated course, we unconsciously push our civilization at a faster and faster pace toward its doom.

2. Unless otherwise indicated, quotations from Scripture are from *The New English Bible*, © The Delegates of the Oxford University Press and The Syndics of the Cambridge University Press 1961, 1970.

3. *Life Against Death* (1959), p. 92.

We need a fresh start. We need to rebuild civilization upon a new foundation. It is not enough that we become fatter. Our world needs a new body; it must be regenerated in the etymological sense of the word—be created again. The old body must die if life is to be preserved in a new one. For man's body is much more than his own limited organism; it is the whole civilization we have created in order to make existence possible. Biblical language affirms that for life to be preserved, the body, which has grown old and senile—which has ceased to be an instrument for the expression of life and now functions to repress it—must be dissolved. It has to die. This is what gives life a chance to create a new body for itself. It is then resurrected in another form. Society, organization, civilization, culture: these are our limbs, the extensions of our biological structure. They have become oppressive and repressive: they act counter to the groaning of life for freedom and expression. The faster they grow, the greater the repression. This body must be dissolved, if life is to have a chance to create a new one. We have to go through death and resurrection. We need to be born again.

To let this body die is to dissolve the rules of life as they have been established by past generations. The dead must not rule the world of the living. And only beyond the dissolution of the old, now hopelessly enmeshed in its internal contradictions, can a new synthesis be created.

Animals are unable do this. They cannot recreate their bodies. They have to play the game of life to the very end, even if —as with the lemmings—it becomes a suicidal enterprise. With man things are different. His body is larger than his organism. He thus has a fantastic and unique chance to let go of an old pattern of life in order to create a new one. He survives by a literal process of death and resurrection. This is what it means to be creative. This is what it means to be free. He is not condemned to carry out to their final, insane consequences the mistakes his ancestors have committed. There is nothing, absolutely nothing, that says the present organization of life must be his fate. New experiments are possible. Life *may* begin again.

Am I a romantic visionary, without a sufficient sense of reality? I do not think so. Indeed, the first time this idea struck me was not while studying the Bible or reading poetry. The logic of death and resurrection began to make sense for me when I read Thomas S. Kuhn's *The Structure of Scientific Revolutions*.[4]

Some of us have the vague idea that scientific knowledge is a homogeneous body which has grown up without interruption or discontinuity. According to Kuhn, however, things happen in a totally different way. Very often scientific investigation reaches an impasse. New problems arise which cannot be solved by the logic which has been in use up to that moment. No matter how hard the scientist tries, the solutions elude his efforts. When this happens, Kuhn points out, one thing is obvious: the prevailing scientific paradigm has become inadequate. If the new problem is to be solved, the old logic has to be abandoned and the scientist must strike out along a new line. If he sticks to the old one, we will find here something similar to Forrester's law: however hard he works, the problem becomes increasingly more absurd and complicated. According to Kuhn, therefore, science moves ahead not through a homogeneous and uninterrupted process of growth, but rather through revolutionary events in which the dominant models are abandoned and new ones invented.

Kuhn perceived that the validity of his thesis reached far beyond the domain of science. For the historical fact is that social organization itself is always going through a process of

4. 1966.

dissolution and rebuilding. "Just as scientific revolutions are inaugurated by a growing sense that the existing paradigm has ceased to function adequately," Kuhn remarks, "political revolutions are inaugurated by a growing sense that the existing institutions have ceased adequately to meet the problems posed by an environment that they have in part created." When modular imagination exhausts its possibilities, the time for creative imagination has arrived. But the similarity is deeper still. "Political revolutions aim to change political institutions in ways that those institutions themselves prohibit."[5] Which means that the creative act must necessarily be considered absurd, insane, irresponsible, heretical, or subversive by the Organization it proposes to supersede.

The same thing may be said of ourselves as individuals. Consciousness is to behavior what paradigms are for scientific research. It is a model according to which we structure our experience. What we call personality is indeed the specific form of psychic organization we have engendered in the course of our personal stories. People who have lived in situations of great social stability are able to go through life without ever feeling that their personal syntheses were being challenged. From childhood to old age there is a conscious process of growth, development, and maturing. They never experience what has become so common today: the identity crisis. There are conditions, however, which prove more complicated than our means of organizing them. Zorba used to say that he was too big for the world. Few of us have that feeling today. We sense just the opposite: that the world is too big for us, too complicated. Indeed, the problem is not one of size, but rather of *being able to make sense* of what exists. The world does not make sense.

When we come to this conclusion we are simply confessing

5. *Ibid.*, pp. 91–92.

that the data of our experience refuse to be put together in the ways to which we are accustomed. We have arrived at an impasse. This situation is exactly the same as that of the scientist who discovers that his new problem cannot be solved by means of his old theoretical model. It is the moment of identity crisis: our taken-for-granted personal structure falls apart. What can we do? One solution is to stick to the old identity and close one's eyes to the world. But this is literally to stop living, for life is relation and experience. The price of preserving our past identity is to bring life to a standstill. The other possibility is to allow the "old man" to die, so that a new one may be born. This is "new birth." There is no continuity in the process. Our body remains apparently the same, and we know it must be the same person. But very often we come to love what we have hated and to hate what we have loved. We have not grown; we have not simply matured. We have gone through death and resurrection.

Human life has a logic all its own. When it comes to certain crises where past experience no longer helps it to move ahead, but rather makes progress impossible, it leaves the past behind and starts afresh. This, as I understand it, is the essence of the creative act, so tersely summarized by Harold Rugg. "The key to the nature of the creative act," he says, "lay in *giving up long held presuppositions* and *in beginning again with a new orientation.*"[6] This is what imagination is all about.

Creativity, however, is a forbidden act. The Organization of our world is essentially sterile and hates anything that could be the seed of regeneration. New life is outside the limits of its space and opposed to its rules; thus the creative act takes place almost totally underground. And this is an undesired pregnancy. Remembering Revelation, "The dragon stands in front of the woman who is about to give birth, so that when her child

6. *Imagination* (1963), p. 289. (Emphasis supplied.)

is born he may devour it," one might say. We do not know whether the child will be aborted before it is born or consumed after it has seen the light of day.

Blacks are part of this pregnancy. For centuries they were nothing more than pawns in the chess game of the white man. They had no future. They belonged to their masters. Some substantial improvements could be made without changing the rules: they could move up in the game—perhaps to the status of knights or castles. For a while they were fascinated by the idea. Centuries of brainwashing had made them believe that to be good is to be white. Since they could not become Whites they could at least behave as Whites do and gain their respect and confidence. This was the dream of integration. And that was all right with the Whites. Their game was not being challenged. Business was to go on as usual, maybe better. Integrated Blacks were likely to improve their patterns of conspicuous consumption so as to keep up with their new status. But they perceived the trap. And suddenly they realized that in order to become whole, they had to abandon the white man's game and create their own.

The same dynamic is hidden in what we call the youth rebellion or the generation gap. This last expression is deceptive. It reduces the differences between young and old to a question of time. One assumes that once the young become "mature" the gap will disappear. However, beneath this process is the new awareness that adults are those who have been determining how the game of life is to be played. The young are discovering that there must be something radically wrong with a process of education that prepares them for a game they do not want to play. The youth rebellion is a protest against this condition and the expression of a will to live life, not according to the rules inherited from dead generations, but according to values and aspirations they themselves are creating.

The poor nations of the world, with their banners of national-ism and self-determination—what are these if not rebellion on the part of the oppressed and their refusal to move ahead according to the logic of the oppressor?

Do we not find the same creative act announcing itself in Women's Lib? The search for a new identity is the positive side of women's rejection of our institutional and cultural arrangements, which have sacralized men as sources of power and wisdom, reducing women to the condition of objects, functions, and ornaments of a game whose rules were established by males. In all these instances we see the same creative process taking place: long-held presuppositions are given up as one tries to begin again with a new orientation.

These are parables of what should be taking place in our whole civilization, and an indictment of the absolute incapacity, on the part of Organization, to move beyond its own weird derangement. Do we have an ecological problem? How are we to put an end to it? The dinosaur anwers: by getting bigger. We must invent new devices to stop pollution. A new line of production is created. A new market is opened. New possibilities of profit appear. Economy grows. A patch of unshrunk cloth is sewn on to the old coat.

We act as if it were possible to stop pollution by speeding up the very mechanisms that produce it. But the solution is at the opposite end of the scale. We will be saved, not by becoming bigger but by becoming smaller. Unlimited growth must give place to an economy of scarcity. We must bring the process of production and consumption to a minimum; otherwise we will perish.

Do we have the problem of war? How can we reverse the trend? The dinosaur answers: by getting bigger. We ignore the fact that we cannot abolish the absurdity of power by increasing power! But the solution, instead, is to be found in that ultimate "madness" so beautifully described by Nietzsche.

And perhaps the great day will come when a people, distinguished by wars and victories and by the highest development of a military order and intelligence, and accustomed to make the heaviest sacrifices for these things, will exclaim of its own free will, "We break the sword," and will smash its entire military establishment down to its lowest foundations. Rendering oneself unarmed when one had been the best-armed, out of a height of feeling—that is the means to real peace, which must always rest on a peace of mind; whereas the so-called armed peace, as it now exists in all countries, is the absence of peace of mind. One trusts neither oneself nor one's neighbor and, half from hatred, half from fear, does not lay down arms. Rather perish than hate and perish, and twice rather perish then make oneself hated and feared—this must someday become the highest maxim for every single commonwealth too.[7]

Mistakes are an important part of our experience. If we recognize our mistakes, we will no longer repeat them. The trouble with nature was that it could not correct the mistake it made in creating the dinosaur, which therefore had to perish.

There is nothing basically wrong with making mistakes. But to make impossible their correction—this is nothing less than sheer insanity. Yet it is what our civilization has done. It took a mistaken experiment, an experiment which is enmeshed in ever worse contradictions, and made of it the ultimate criterion by which sanity is to be measured. To be sane is to agree with the system; to disagree is to show the folly of madness.

Psychoanalysis has provided the ethicoreligious legitimation of the system. "By assuming that avoidance, rejection or resistance is an abnormal phenomenon, it condemns as neurotic the effort to maintain a system of values, and would sacrifice these values in favor of a goal of mere social conformity." "The normal person, presumably, if there were a normal person, would

7. Friedrich Nietzsche, *The Wanderer and His Shadow*, in Walter Kaufmann, ed., *The Portable Nietzsche* (1968), p. 72.

find fault with nothing and accept everything."[8] Who is healthy? Who is not? How does the psychiatrist go about finding the answer to these questions? "Well," answers Thomas Szasz, "Disraeli was once asked to define an agreeable gentleman, and he said: 'A gentleman who agrees with me.' In the same way, a normal person is one whose beliefs and conduct coincide with those of the examining psychiatrist."[9] And since the still repressed collective unconscious of our civilization takes for granted that present Organization is reality, it has to define social deviation as sickness. It is not surprising that the Soviet regime has developed a policy of getting rid of dissenting thought by secluding its creators in asylums for the mentally disturbed.

To be dysfunctional is to be bad. To be functional is to be good. As Gunnar Myrdal put it, from the standpoint of the system "if a thing has a 'function' it is good or at least essential."[10] *This is the unconfessed metaphysics of realism:* the system is the measure of everything. It judges everything, but nothing is qualified to judge it.

And this is its unconfessed anthropology: man is a function of the social structure. Man, therefore, is judged by the system. The system is his law. It establishes the coordinates of the order in which he lives. The system provides the stimuli. Man reacts with the adequate responses.

One thing only is forgotten: that what is called reality was created by man. Man is the creator. The social system is the creature. Therefore man, and not the system, is the measure of everything. It is not man who is to be judged by comparing him to the system. The system itself is under the judgment of man.

8. Prescott Lecky, *Self-Consistency: A Theory of Personality* (1961), p. 123.
9. Maggie Scarf, "Normality is a Square Circle or a Four-Sided Triangle," (1971), p. 40.
10. *An American Dilemma* (1944), II, p. 1056.

So imagination is not to be declared unbalanced for disagreeing with the facts of "reality." It is reality that must be declared mad when it does not agree with the aspirations of imagination. The modern reversal of appropriate order which is the very essence of realism is due to a sort of amnesia as to the origins of the human world. *It totally ignores the fact that our human world is the result of creative acts.* And there is no creative act without imagination. How can the creature rebel against its creator? Is not this the essence of idolatry?

I want to propose, therefore, a new paradigm for understanding the conditions of human life. In the beautiful phrase of Paul Lehmann, our problem is to find out "what it takes to make and to keep human life human in the world." We must start with imagination, for this is the prerequisite of the creative act. And the creative act is the highest expression of human life.

But we must not do what Freud did, in applying the pattern of present reality to creations of the imagination and dismissing them as sickness. Imagination is the mother of creativity. We will understand it when we understand how it speaks of the child that is growing in its womb.

5

The Magical Intention of Imagination

The sign on the wall said FAST FOR PEACE.

I started asking myself what difference there is between "fast for peace" and "dance for rain"? I could not find any. There is as much relation between the act of dancing and rain as there is between the act of fasting and the achievement of peace. Magical acts. But since I could not avoid loving the hands that wrote those words, I refused to dismiss them as sheer nonsense.

In Czechoslovakia a student burned himself to death during the Russian invasion. In Vietnam Buddhist monks have done the same. Like the "fast for peace," these are magical acts. Human ashes have no power over the living. Magical acts, without any pragmatic logic. But because I could not help feeling a part of the suffering that led these people to deeds of such finality, I refused to dismiss them as waste and stupidity.

I was in the barbershop when the old woman came. She was obviously poor, a marginal outcast without any economic function in society. She wanted to buy a lottery ticket: one dollar for a hundred thousand! Here again, between the buying of the ticket and the winning of the prize there is as much causal connection as between dancing and rain. (The rain dancer, ironically, has better chances of winning than she did.) Nobody thinks of a lottery as state-sponsored magic. Yet the psychic mechanism that leads man to perform magic is the same as led the old lady to buy the ticket. And because I also am a human being, I could not dismiss her act as folly.

Magic is the oldest impulse of the human soul. Perhaps because it is also the deepest. They myth of the fall tells us how the snake deceived man by suggesting to him that he could become the Supreme Magician by eating the fruit of the tree. "You will be like God" (Gen. 3:5, RSV). It is quite significant that the myth does not say that the desire in itself was sinful. Man is not expelled from paradise because of his magical aspirations, but because of his alliance with the Deceiver. And as Goethe shows in the tragedy of Faust, one cannot attain freedom by giving up freedom.

The interpretation of magic is crucial for our purposes, just as the interpretation of dreams is crucial for psychoanalysis. Magic is imagination taking hold of the body; imagination is the secret form of magic. Sartre has remarked that "the act of imagination is a magical one. It is an incantation, destined to produce the object of one's thought, the thing one desires, in a manner that one can take possession of it."[1] And conversely, Feuerbach observes that "the power of miracle is nothing else than the power of the imagination."[2] The fate of imagination and magic are thus inextricably related. If it can be proved that magic is irrational and dysfunctional, there is no way of avoiding the conclusion that imagination, too, is irrational and dysfunctional.

Freud understood this connection very clearly. According to

1. Jean Paul Sartre, *The Psychology of Imagination* (1968), p. 159.
2. Ludwig Feuerbach, *The Essence of Christianity* (1957), p. 130.

him, they are different expressions of a single process in our mental life. Thus the criteria and methods to be used for the interpretation of one must be employed in interpreting the other. As the reader will recall, Freud's theory of neurosis says that man becomes mentally ill because he refuses to accept reality as it is. He tries to escape. And because there is nowhere else to go, he builds a world in his imagination where his desires are sustained and fulfilled. The neurotic is thus a person who endows his wishes with the status of reality, and by the same token tries to abolish reality itself by wishing it away. He is thus a magician: he creates what does not exist, *ex nihilo,* and dissolves what is into nothing. But how does he accomplish this? Simply by thinking and desiring, or more precisely, by thinking his desires. The primordial tool with the help of which the neurotic creates and annihilates is the thinking process itself. As Freud put it, he believes in the "omnipotence of thought."[3]

It is this belief that unites the neurotic and his imagination with magic—for the magician is above all one who acts as if reality could be changed by means of consciousness. As Frazer has pointed out, "Men mistook the order of their ideas for the order of nature, and hence imagined that the control that they have, or seem to have, over their thoughts, permitted them to have a corresponding control over things."[4] The magician, according to this interpretation, would be someone who believes that the world can be created by the power of the word: the father of idealism!

It took a long time for man to find the key to deciphering his dreams. Because their plots and symbols do not follow the logic of our conscious life, it was assumed that they were devoid of meaning, and they were thus discarded as lacking significance for interpreting the human condition. It was Freud who

3. *Totem and Taboo* (1946), p. 111.
4. Quoted by Freud, *ibid.,* p. 108.

showed that this was not true. They have a meaning, a logic, and a wisdom. For their apparent absurdity to become meaningful, one has only to discover the key that will unlock them. And what is this key? Dreams have their roots in the existential situation of man. They are symptoms of the conditions he experiences, a code in which he speaks of himself and tells his secret. So, to discover the message of dreams one has to understand the life that has given them birth.

Imagination is to society what dreams are to the individual. In every utopia, in every work of art, in every religious fantasy and magic ritual, society is telling its hidden feelings. It speaks of its frustrations and aspirations and unveils the repressed yearnings that cannot be articulated in common language. Like dreams, they seem meaningless at first glance. We try to arrive at their meaning through the logic of our common sense, and all we get is nonsense. We must find the key that unlocks their secret.

This is what we must have in mind as we approach the sphere of magic and its twin brother, imagination. Strange as it may appear, Freud did not see this. If in his interpretation of dreams he transcended the limits of realism, superseding the assumptions of his civilization, in his interpretation of magic he remained strictly within its canons of logic. And what are these? That the function of thought is to describe objective reality, while the purpose of action is to manipulate it. These are the basic dogmas of our scientific-technological era. Thus, if the descriptions are inaccurate or the action ineffective, they are dismissed as wrong. Freud, accepting these assumptions, measures magic as if its intention were scientific and technological and concludes that it does not pass the test of the reality principle.

This interpretation presents a number of problems. Our behavior is governed by certain pragmatic criteria. We tend to abandon modes of thought and courses of action which do not prove adequate for the solution of our problems. As Berger and Luckmann point out, "The validity of my knowledge of everyday life is taken for granted by myself and by others until further notice, that is, until a problem arises that cannot be solved in terms of it."[5] But if so, man should have become disillusioned with magic long ago. Yet this did not happen. In spite of its practical failures, he continued to cherish it. How can one account for this?

Before ball-point pens were invented, we used fountain pens. We still use them, but there is no doubt that the former are more practical. Further back in time, we remember when we wrote with a pen point attached to a holder. And before that there was the age of the quill. In the logic of technology the simpler and more effective displaces the less simple and less effective. Now let us accept for a moment that magic is a primitive technology. What should have happened to it, with the advent of modern techniques? It should have been reduced to a museum piece, just like the quill. But this did not occur. The logic of the "omnipotence of thought" continues to inspire man, to create visions, to give birth to movements, and to shape lives.

Whether we like it or not, magic goes on making history. The new importance of the word "consciousness" in common language is in itself an indication of how fascinated we are with the possibility that reality can be changed by means of thought. According to Roszak, for instance, this is the basic intention of the counter-culture movement: to explore the *politics of consciousness.*[6] And is there any other reason for the fascination that *The Greening of America* has exerted upon large segments of the American population? It is a book about magic. It proclaims

5. Peter Berger and Thomas Luckmann, *The Social Construction of Reality* (1967), p. 44.
6. Theodore Roszak, *The Making of a Counter-Culture* (1969), p. 156.

the transformation of the world by means of a transformation of consciousness. Traditional politics is no longer necessary. A new future is being engendered by a consciousness informed by love. The explosion of art, the drug scene, the unusual longing for religious experiences—these are all expressions of man's effort to abolish reality and create a new one through the power of the mind. And even those who do not indulge in these magical rituals cannot avoid their occurrence in the realm of mind. Imagination itself is magic. Whenever we daydream, whenever we name our desires, whenever we move beyond the closed circle of the reality that imprisons us, our consciousness is operating out of the magic aspirations that control its dynamics.

Is it possible to understand magic in a different way, so that we can discover the secret it both hides and reveals? Is it possible to rescue imagination from the indictment of insanity? Can we penetrate beyond the apparent lack of realism and absurdity of magic and imagination, to enter into the thus-far-hidden wisdom of their function, as Freud did with dreams? What is at stake is the very wisdom of evolution itself. Otherwise, how can we account for the fact that animals are perfect realists, whereas man, in a stage of higher complexity in the evolutionary scale, cannot rid himself of this strange obsession with magic and imagination?

Why does man create magic? The answer is the key to our riddle. Suppose that instead we were simply interested in descriptive details. No matter how precise the picture, we could not avoid looking at it from the standpoint of the dominant categories of our culture. We would find it ridiculous and primitive. Its secret would remain hidden from us. The same is true of dreams. It is not enough to remember their images and sequence. One must ask, why did this man unconsciously create this dream? Only then do we begin to discover its intrinsic relation to life, and therewith its meaning.

Why does man create magic? Malinowski was intrigued by the fact that when natives of the Trobriand Islands were to fish in the inner lagoon there were no magical ceremonies for the occasion. The situation changed, however, when they had to go out to sea. Now the whole process was carefully prepared by magic. Why? The reason was simple. In the lagoon they had a sense of self-assurance and control. There was no danger. Their lives were not being risked. The deep sea, however, took their self-confidence away. The game was dangerous. They were gambling their lives. In one situation they had a sense of power, in the other a feeling of impotence. His conclusion, therefore, was that man practices magic when he feels he lacks power to carry out his intention by means of his own resources.[7]

The difference between Freud and Malinowski is radical. For Freud, magic comes from man's illusion of omnipotence. For Malinowski what is found underneath magic is the realizaton of impotence. Man is involved in action. So long as it is effective in producing the desired results, there is no problem. But suddenly he is stopped. An obstacle brings his activity to a halt; his intention is frustrated. He realizes something quite painful: the power of his arms is inadequate to carry out the commands of his heart. He experiences reality as it is, something that goes against the direction of his will.

Realism would dictate: Accept fate. If you are impotent, there is nothing to be done. But man refuses. "My impotence I acknowledge, but my desires I will not yield!" He refuses to allow action to be imprisoned in his shortcomings. So, if on the one hand he realizes his impotence, "yet his desire grips him only more strongly."[8]

The alternatives are simple. Either to be caged within the narrow limits of reality and respond properly to its stimuli, or

7. Bronislaw Malinowski, *Magic, Science and Religion* (1948), p. 79.
8. *Ibid.*

to act by the vision of one's intention. In the one case behavior is determined by the present. Man adapts himself. In the other, he acts out of a passion for something absent, and has therefore to refuse the verdict of the present. Thus Malinowski finds that magic is an expression of hope. In it the "organism reproduces the acts suggested by the anticipation of hope."[9] We imitate the shape of hope. We attempt to give birth to it, to make it incarnate, to transform the absent into the present. One is literally possessed by it. If we remember that human action is essentially a pursuit of values, then we find that behind the culture-creating act and magic one single dynamic is at work.

As in dreams, so in magic consciousness reveals its own secrets. Wherever reality makes it impossible for man to create with his hands the desire of his heart, he nevertheless affirms, preserves, and lives his aspirations by means of symbolic action. This "has subjectively all the value of a real action, to which emotion would, if not impeded, naturally have led."[10] Thus magic cannot be classified with the hoe, the hammer, and the saw, but rather with art, dialogue, laughing and crying. Its intention is not to describe how the world is, but to declare how it should be, according to the exigencies of personality. It is an expression of those feelings, intentions, and hopes which are the very foundations of everything a man does.

Freud's conclusion is that magic is the result of insanity, a residue of the primitive attitudes of an irrational animal which has not yet come to terms with reality. But according to our interpretation, on the contrary, magic reveals the basic intention of personality. It is not an accidental mistake, but rather something "based on a universal psycho-physiological mechanism."[11] It carries with it the ego's endless search for a world

9. *Ibid.*
10. *Ibid.*, pp. 80–81.
11. *Ibid.*, p. 80.

to love. Its abolition would imply the very dissolution of personality as we know it. Man performs magic because inside himself he has a magical intention: things as they are must be dissolved, and a new world, expressive of love, must take their place. Without the magical intention, culture could not have been created. For culture comes into being as a result of man's refusal to accept the world as it is, and as an expression of his utopian dream of creating an *ordo amoris*.

Magic is a flower that grows only in impotence. This is rather revealing. Those who enjoy power sense that things are under their control. They feel safe. Their heart has found satisfactions in things as they are, and as a consequence their consciousness has become adapted to the status quo. As we have seen, their intention is not to abolish but to preserve "reality." This is the hidden secret of their realism: things must remain unchanged. When man feels, on the contrary, that his intentions are frustrated and his desires repressed by the dominant order, of necessity a magical intention will arise. Why? Because of the very dynamics of consciousness. It must live in a world that makes sense. And a world which denies the aspirations of man as insane does not make sense.

As I remarked earlier, an awareness of meaning only exists when we feel that reality is expressive of and intrumental for the heart. When this is not so, personality finds itself surrounded by an alien world and is in danger of plunging into chaos. In order to remain whole, it must preserve the sense of power. It must believe that the world is controlled by its intention. But if reality in fact makes this impossible, then consciousness itself creates magic as the only means whereby it can keep itself whole. Magic is not, therefore, the behavior of the insane; it is rather personality trying to preserve itself in the midst of an impersonal world which does not make sense. If magical behavior seems senseless, it is because it represents the object one aspires to without actually creating it. But when we move beyond this superficial level into its unarticulated meaning we hear something quite different. The absurdity of magic is really the absurdity of the situation that demands it, by making the real act of creation impossible and so reducing man to impotence.

There is a growing concern in this country about the alarming incidence of drug addiction among GIs in Vietnam. It is indeed rather strange, since if there is anyone who should be totally committed to the dominant order of things it is the soldier. By renouncing his own power of decision, he accepts the fact that his body, behavior, life, and even death are equally at the disposal of the military hierarchy. Drug addiction represents a fateful blow to this assumption. Why does one resort to drugs? Because of their magical power. They make it possible to move away from the senseless situation in which one is trapped, toward a more rewarding world. Whenever one is forced to do what is meaningless one is on the verge of insanity. One might rebel and say No. But soldiers cannot do this; it is treason. They have to go on, to march every day toward what is absurd, and do with their hands what looks like madness. How can one expect a soldier to remain sober, with high morale? It is not possible to stay sane in a situation that is fundamentally insane. The absurdity of drug addiction, therefore, is nothing in itself. One will never understand it by simply asking, "What's wrong with our GIs?" There is nothing wrong with them. The absurdity of drug addiction is the absurdity of their impotence in an insane situation.

It is rather significant that the politics of consciousness, with all its polymorphous manifestations, follows a decade of intense revolutionary expectations and frustrations. The oppressed believed they had the power to carry out their aspirations. They trusted their action as an instrument for the creation of a new society. But they were defeated. Reality stopped them. Man refuses to give up his dreams. How are his hopes to survive? By being acted out in life. And when this happens, magic is born. Behavior that invokes magic is a symptom of repression and control; it indicates that the order of power does not make room for fulfilling the intentions of the heart.

Thus magic is neither primitive science nor technology. Its intention is not descriptive. It is both *the realization of the impotence of desire vis-à-vis a certain reality, and at the same time the affirmation of the axiological priority of these same desires over the reality that denies them.* If we are to decipher its secret we must realize that its intention is ethical. Cassirer once remarked that "the ethical world is never given; it is forever in the making. To live in the ideal world," he concludes, quoting Goethe, "is to treat the impossible as if it were possible."[12] But is not this what magic is all about? Certainly it looks like folly. But why? Because it acts out of its vision of hope: it gives a higher significance to what seems impossible (from the perspective of the present) than to the brute facts themselves. According to its logic, reality has no right. (Here might must not be identified with right.) Magic embodies and gives shape in the present to aspirations which the present itself abhors. Freud was wrong. Magic is a theory neither of the omnipotence of thought nor of the omnipotence of desire. On the contrary, it is an acknowledgment that reality is not moved by our desires, *but that it ought to be.* It gives bodily form to what Ernst Bloch enunciated in the word: "What is, cannot be true." Facts are not values. Therefore facts themselves must be overcome.

Magic thus displays the very structure of the creative act— it *is* the creative act as aborted by the dominant powers: a fetus, a projection struggling to remain alive. Indeed, what does it do?

12. Ernst Cassirer, *An Essay on Man* (1953), p. 85.

It refuses to accept the rules of the game of reality. Those presuppositions of thought and behavior which are sanctified as canons of realism are abandoned. And at the same time it affirms a new possibility.

Why is it that magic seems so absurd? Because it is the reflection of an absurd situation. It speaks at the same moment of the necessity and the impossibility of the creative act. A creative act is needed because reality goes against the aspirations of man by making him impotent, thus undermining the very conditions of his wholeness. At the same time the creative act is made impossible by the simple fact that the dominant reality is stronger.

This is an impossible situation. There is no way out. Society is trapped in the logic of the dinosaur. Magic thus has a prophetic significance, since it proclaims by its very absurdity that for human wholeness and social regeneration to take place, the existing conditions of power which make this impossible must be abolished. *But magic does not have power to fulfill the truth of its insight and intention.* Behind it we find a powerless man. The truth of magic will become reality only when his impotence turns to power.

6

The Playful Intention of Imagination

Adults, always and everywhere, take their values for granted. No one ever doubts that the adult style of life and the adult world are superior to those of children. Children are weak. They have no means to defend themselves against the facts of power. Because they are systematically defeated, we assume that our power to force our values upon children is evidence that our way of defining reality is truer or more human than theirs. The processes called socialization and education are programs whereby we impose our reality on the weak—namely, children—through a subtle brainwashing process or a not-so-subtle exercise of physical and psychological coercion. We want them to become adults. They must be made to fit into the little boxes (whether houses or values) we have built for ourselves.

Why do we do this? Because if we are to preserve our world, children must play the game of life according to our rules. So they are socialized—that is, their imagination and aspirations are controlled and defined by ourselves. When we succeed, we say they have become mature. What does this word really mean, as we use it in our common language? Peter Berger has a delightful paragraph on this point. "Maturity," he says, "is a state of mind that has settled down, come to terms with the status quo, given up the wilder dreams of adventure and fulfillment."[1] It is this settled-down state of affairs that defines the dynamics of the adult world.

What is a child? What—for a child—defines the rules of the game? The myth of the innocence and purity of children has long been dead. Children are not pure. For one thing, we do not know what purity means. Nor are they full of love. What is it that characterizes a child? I would like to make a suggestion— no more than a suggestion. I agree with biblical anthropology in its indication that man is to be understood by what he does. His activity defines the circle of his humanity. If this is true, what is the typical activity of children? The answer is very simple. Children *play*.

What is play?

Play is nonproductive activity. It does not aim at the production of any object.

But why then do children play, if it does not produce anything? Again the answer is simple. Play does not produce objects, but it delivers pleasure. If you find this word too charged with hedonistic overtones you may substitute "joy." This sounds more pious. Perhaps the nature of play will be clarified if we remember the distinction made by Augustine between *things which are to be used* and *things which are to be enjoyed*. When I use something it is always a means to something else, a tool for my productive activity, whether I am using words, things, or persons. When I enjoy something, on the other hand, it is always an end in itself. This is what play is all about: it is an end in itself, it is for the purpose of enjoyment, it produces pleasure.

1. *Invitation to Sociology* (1963), p. 55.

Clearly pleasure is the determining principle of a child's life. Bergson comments, not without nostalgia: "What a childhood we should have had if only we had been left to do as we pleased!"[2] Freud points in the same direction when he suggests that the most primordial drive in life is the pleasure principle. Children believe in the *omnipotence of desire,* and they organize their world and act according to this perspective. They abandon pleasure as their guiding principle only under the repression of the "mature" world. Play, as an activity which is an end in itself, is nothing less than an expression of this fundamental search for pleasure. And it is only because it produces pleasure that it does not need to exhibit any objective product to justify itself.

It was this fact that led Freud to identify the dynamics of play with the dynamics of magic. According to him, in magic man rests satisfied with a simple "representation of the gratified wish." And this "is altogether comparable to the *play* of children." "If play and imitative representation suffice for the child and for primitive man," he adds, "it must not be taken as a sign of modesty, in our sense, or of resignation due to the realization of their impotence; on the contrary, it is the very obvious result of the excessive valuation of their wish."[3] According to his interpretation, they are thus nothing less than diverse expressions of neurotic behavior, that is, behavior not yet reconciled with reality. The neurotic, like the child and the magician, finds pleasure in a construct of the imagination and not in a real thing. Once again our paradigm must be tested. The question is, which is the higher logic, the reality principle that represses play or the pleasure principle that creates it? The question is whether play is simply "kid stuff"—a bit of irrationality which we permit in the midst of the adult world—or whether through

2. Henri Bergson, *The Two Sources of Morality and Religion* (1935), p. 1.
3. Sigmund Freud, *Totem and Taboo,* p. 110.

play children are revealing the very wisdom of imagination, still free of the distortions of our adult life.

There is no way of denying that the logic of play implies a radical negation of the dominant logic of modern adult society, which accepts as its central dogma that man is justified by his products. His humanity is defined by his function, which in turn is defined by the dominant structure of power. Ours is a world controlled by two poles: production and consumption. The best of anything—whether a man, a machine, or a social system—is the one that produces the greatest number of objects. And the degree of self-realization (here comes its "mature" humanistic philosophy!) is measured by the power to consume. I remember an old missionary who claimed to have found the ultimate solution for the Communist problem. It would suffice, he said, to print enough copies of the Sears Roebuck catalog and distribute them behind the Iron Curtain. Obviously, what he had in mind was that no other economic system could match such a display of power to produce and ability to consume.

For of course the more one produces, the more one is able to consume; and the more one consumes, the greater must be the actual production. Man is a thing-eating animal: only mouth and stomach. This is what we call prosperity. The criterion for the judgment of the well-being of peoples and even of their achievement of humanity and happiness is how much they are able to produce. Thus we have divided the world between the developed and the underdeveloped nations. We take for granted that the great task is to bridge the gap between them. What this means, really, is that we look at the world from the logic of a production-consumption society, a society which believes that action is justified by its product. Is this not the form which justification by works takes in our modern world?

It seems to me that this logic is at the root of the cruelty of our society. Once action is only a means to an end, what happens in the action itself does not matter, provided the ends are those determined by our social system. So it does not matter if hundreds of thousands are killed, it does not matter if human beings are destroyed by torture, it does not matter if the powerful force their will upon the weak. What matters is that these actions improve our economy, create the stability we need, preserve our "security." The nature of an action does not matter. The important thing is the product.

Life, however, is not a means to something, but always an end in itself. It was not given to us for the purpose of something beyond it, but rather simply to live abundantly! Is not this the meaning of justification by faith: that we must refuse to measure life in terms of something it produces? What radical consequences this old theological insight would have if we were to appraise our social existence by its logic. Our society, dominated as it is by the dogma of productivity, is the grave of the child and therefore the end of play, since the expansion of things produced and consumed depends on the repression of man's drive toward enjoyment. Thus play implies and does involve a radical critique of this society and the subversion of its values.

I am sure that you have noticed how children are serious about the roles they assume in their play. Nevertheless, they never forget that they are playing. They do not confuse, as adults do, cultural reality with natural reality. The role is not permanent. It is not my essence. It is not ontologized.

"Let's play cowboys and Indians! Today I'll be a cowboy . . . Tomorrow I'll be an Indian!"

Children are aware that they are at the same time actors and authors of the script. Consequently they are free in their script: free to change it, to adapt roles, to throw it away and look for another. They preside over the social organization that play creates—are not its pawns. Children, consequently, are not

committed to preserving the present organization of the structure of play. Every tomorrow is a new beginning, a new reorganization.

A number of factors suggest that play is not peculiar to children but, like magic, an intrinsic element in human activity.
Take, for instance, the idea of "role" in sociology. What it suggests is that society is a drama or comedy which plays itself out
with adults assuming roles as children do. Or take another sociological concept, that of "definition of situation": that a social
situation *is* as it is defined by those who participate in it. But this
is exactly what happens in play! Huizinga in his *Homo Ludens*
goes even further, contending that play cannot be understood
as one among other data of culture. "Here," he says, "we have
to do with an absolutely primary category of life."[4] It is not
culture that produces play but rather play that produces culture. This is why culture itself cannot be understood at all ex-
cept *sub specie ludi.* Indeed, if in the culture-creating act we
find man attempting to set up an *ordo amoris*, and if in play we
find him trying to produce a pleasure-delivering order, we cannot avoid the conclusion that they are expressions of single
dynamic.

If the play of adults is similar to that of children, then what
are the differences between them?

Children, as I have indicated, are always conscious that they
not only assume the roles but write the script as well. They
remember the human origins of their games and always feel
free to abolish them. They remain masters over the situation,
which means that it can be reorganized at will. They set a
pattern of social organization in which structures are to be
defined by man's freedom.

Adults equally assume roles. But they do not remember that

4. Johan Huizinga, *Homo Ludens* (1955), p. 3.

that game has been created by persons; they forget its human origins. And as a consequence they tend to accept it as fate. They *become* what they do. They do not create roles, and are therefore not the authors of their stage directions. Instead of being masters over the situation, they are mastered by it. Play becomes ontology—serious business which cannot be changed. It is baptized as "truth" and "reality." Once man defines his play as reality, he starts acting to force others to become realists —that is, to play according to the rules of his game.

Moreover, if his world is the truth, it must be preserved for tomorrow. A genuine tomorrow cannot occur—if it implies the reorganization of today. The future is defined as a time in which today's organization is preserved and repeated. And still more: once my world is defined as truth, all those who do not want to play my game are, by definition, subversive. Was not this what happened to Jesus?

Things become clearer by means of images.

Children are playing. One of them points his finger at the other and says, "Bang, I killed you!"

Adults are playing. One of them points his gun at the other, and bang: "I killed you!"

Children's play ends with the universal resurrection of the dead. Adult's play ends with universal burial. Whereas the resurrection is the paradigm of the world of children, the world of adults creates the cross.

You may wish to call my attention to the fact that play can easily become alienation. You are right. Indeed, one of the contradictions of our time is that a society dominated by the logic of production and consumption, the negation of play, is precisely the one to present itself as uniquely able to deliver play—*as one of its products of consumption.* It brags about its power to transform the world into a playground (though admission is required . . .). But play is no longer play. It has ceased to be an act of denial of the adult world. It is no longer a debunking activity which points to new possibilities of life. It is now a product of the consumption society. No one can ignore how frequently TV advertises toys. The system of production is seeing to it that the ability to play becomes identified with the need to buy new toys. As Toffler remarked with pleasure, Mattel is educating the girls of today for the adult world of tomorrow. Thus goes the institutional therapy: magic is resolved into technology and play into consumption. What was an act of going beyond, of transcending the rules of reality, becomes an act of remaining inside: the opiate of the people. Play is now *entertainment* and *distraction*, the filling of empty time, escape from boredom, fun for the dwarfed imagination which cannot give birth to anything.

As with dreams and magic, it is necessary to go behind the self-evident. For the obvious is deceptive. If play is more than nonsense, if it has a psychoanalytical meaning, it is necessary to discover the "universal psycho-physiological mechanism" underlying it. Huizinga remarks that all the prevailing hypotheses about it "start from the assumption that play must serve something which is not play. They attack play directly with the quantitative methods of experimental science without first paying attention to its profoundly aesthetical quality." It is assumed that play is a response to certain stimuli and has an adaptational function to perform. "To each and every one of the above 'explanations' it might very well be objected: 'So far so good, but what actually is the *fun* of playing?' This last named element, the *fun* of playing, resists all analysis, all logical interpretation." "From the point of view of a world wholly determined by the operation of blind forces"—in which there is no freedom, and behavior is to be understood according to the logic of stimuli-response patterns—"play would be altogether superfluous. In play there is something at play which transcends the immediate needs of life and imparts meaning to action. However we may regard it, the very fact that play has a meaning implies a non-materialistic quality in the nature of the thing itself. Play only becomes possible, thinkable and understandable when an influx of *mind* breaks down the absolute determinism of the cosmos."[5]

In play man finds meaning, and therefore fun, precisely in suspending the rules of the game of reality, which makes him serious and tense. Reality is sickening. It produces ulcers and nervous breakdowns. Play, however, creates an order out of imagination and therefore out of freedom. As with magic, here imagination assumes flesh—takes the impossible and treats it as if it were possible. In this, man is telling a secret which the rules of the reality principle declare to be sheer nonsense.

But possibility is a relative category. The limits of the social system define what is possible and what is not. In a society built upon the logic of war, peace is not possible. In an economy based on infinite growth, and therefore endless waste, ecological balance is not possible. These impossibilities, however, only describe for us the limits of the social order that creates them. Play, on the other hand, reveals that beyond the dissolution of reality we find, not chaos, but rather new possibilities. The impossible becomes possible. But this new order is not something already discoverable in the status quo; it is created by imagination—it expresses freedom and assumes that the absolute determinism of the cosmos can be broken.

Huizinga is right. Play is not a means to an end. It delivers pleasure, and that is enough. Like magic, it finds satisfaction in the representation of its object.

But this is not the whole truth. Play has an ethical and prophetic significance. Not because it has this intention, but simply

5. *Ibid.*, pp. 1–3.

because it represents the possibility of a different social order. Play implies a radical denial of the logic of the adult world. In play children do not allow the rules of the so-called real world to control their activity. They set apart space and time, and organize it according to the requirements of their heart. Thus we see arise a social reality, a community, which right in the middle of the adult world stands as a protest against it. Its very existence implies the refusal of children to be organized by our reality. Deeply, unconsciously, children are saying along with the magician, "What is, cannot be true!" And they set out to build a world according to their search for joy. They operate on the assumption of the omnipotence of imagination, and therefore of man's will to create a world which will produce happiness. They are a living indictment of the domestication of our imagination, spellbound by the assumption that action is only justified by its external product.

There comes a time, however, when play is forced to stop. It is interrupted either by a voice or by a clock. The adult world imposes itself. So children learn that play is not "for real." It takes place within a stronger reality which tells them when to begin and when to stop. Children want to define their reality, but as Humpty Dumpty remarked, the question is who is master. And human reality is quite different from play. It has to do with political domination, human control, prosperity, performance, production, and consumption. It has to do with everything that makes us sick, unhappy, perverse, and cruel. But as with magic, those who really play—the children—are impotent. They have no way of carrying out their life project. Every child will become an adult. Every butterfly will become a dinosaur. Play must be displaced. Yet with every new generation of boys and girls the same message is repeated: the impossible possibility of a world open to freedom and joy.

Yes, play looks foolish, just as magic does. Why? Because those who live by the power of their imagination happen to be the "weak" ones. But the real meaning of the foolish imagination of the weak is the insane lack of imagination of the strong. The absurdity of the situation lies not in the "impossible possibility" that imagination speaks of, but rather in the fact that *it is made impossible* precisely by those who have power without imagination. Freedom does not exist. This fact does not make control ethically right. The absence of freedom simply discloses the radical perversion of the order of life that is imposed upon the powerless.

Play, therefore, cannot be carried out as it should be. It reminds us of a world that is still absent. Play has a utopian element in it. Every time it comes to an end and we are forced back into reality, we are reminded that our hearts are powerless. And who can totally celebrate in this situation? When one plays as if reality did not exist, one transforms play into an opiate. There is alienation in the tendencies of the system to reduce play to an object of consumption; but there is just as much alienation in the tendencies of the counter-culture to behave *as if* the facts of brutality and repression did not exist. Play points to a future, gives great joy in its limited space; it creates the hope of freedom for the whole world. Under actual conditions of repression it cannot avoid giving birth to a utopian vision. It works like an *aperitif*, suggesting that although we find ourselves captives of the adult world, this need not be our total fate. There are other possibilities for human life.

Nietzsche was an apologist of play. "I would believe only in a god who could dance," he said. "And when I saw my devil I found him serious, thorough, profound, and solemn: it was the spirit of gravity—through him all things fall."[6] But today the apologists of play, when they quote Nietzsche as their ally, seem

6. Friedrich Nietzsche, *Thus Spoke Zarathustra*, in Walter Kaufmann, ed., *The Portable Nietzsche* (1968), p. 153.

not to have read him as they should. His parable of the transformations of the spirit recounts the origins of play and the conditions under which it is possible. The spirit, he tells us, goes through three metamorphoses. At first it becomes a camel; then the camel becomes a lion; and the lion finally becomes a child. The camel is the passive man, the beast of burden which kneels down, wanting to be well laden. He is impotent, but he does not rebel; he accepts reality as his fate. He has been properly socialized. He is mature and well-adjusted—not free, but he does not want to be free. But then the camel becomes a lion. This is the spirit as it struggles for freedom. It has emerged from impotence and learned the magic words: "I will." It becomes aware that the reality imposed upon him is not reality at all, but simply the creation of the "Great Dragon" which is its master. There is the mighty dragon, covered with golden scales, each representing a value thousands of years old. "All value of all things shines on me," he says. "All value has long been created, and I am all created value. Verily, there shall be no more 'I will.' Thus speaks the dragon."

Is not this voice familiar to us? If new values are going to be created, and if imagination is to transform its hopes into historical reality, the dragon must be killed. Old values must be broken. But for this to be done, the power that upholds them has to be overthrown. Thus a new man is born: the revolutionary. His voice is like thunder. He shouts his anger, his aspirations, his will to break down in order to create. And he gets ready for battle. In Nietzsche's parable the lion kills the dragon, and once the dragon is dead becomes a child. Why? "The child," he says, "is innocence and forgetting, a new beginning, a game . . . a sacred 'Yes.' For the game of creation . . . a sacred 'Yes' is needed."[7]

7. *Ibid.*, pp. 137–39.

How could the camel play? A dancing camel is rather ridiculous! How can the lion play, if the dragon is there with its mighty power? Play only becomes real after the dissolution of oppression. This is why, in Nietzsche, one may and must play *now* only in anticipation of what is to be fulfilled *then*. Play brings the vision of the future, and at the same time makes the experience of unfreedom in the present still more unbearable and cruel. Yes, play! But your play must remind you that there are values to be created. Your playground—be it your commune, your home, your church, whatever it may be—is still under the power of the dragon. How can you dance with freedom in a world which is not free? So make the world free. Destroy the devil of gravity. And then the whole earth will become a free space where the child can create and start anew. Thus play creates the ethical exigency.

In real life (this is our experience today) the end is somewhat different. The only thing broken in the fight is the lion's claws. So the end of the parable has to be rewritten, and would run somewhat like this: "The lion discovered that anger is not an evidence of power, and that 'I will' does not mean 'I can.' And he returned, sad and disappointed, leaving the dragon unscratched. And he began telling his friends that it was no longer necessary to fight the dragon, since it would soon die of an incurable disease. The shouts of anger were no longer needed, the enthusiasm of protest marches and demonstrations vanished, and the cold logic of political analysis was no longer heard. Revolutionaries exchanged their rifles for guitars, and the hardships of theoretical thought for the sweet melody of love songs." Just as it happened long ago with a revolutionary community which expected the coming of a Liberator, the Christian Church— The Liberator did not come, it got tired of waiting and started saying, "He has already come. He is in the midst of us. The war is over. Rejoice and celebrate." They took the bitter herbs of their sacraments, and what was once *aperitif* became an orgy. They despaired of the future of the earth and decided to live in the world of illusions their wishes created.

Play becomes alienation, celebration becomes opiate, and the ethical consciousness is dissolved. Politics is abolished, and one behaves *as if* the unfree world were already free. The dinosaur attempts to fly like the butterfly—and the result is ludicrous.

The intention of play is creativity. As in magic, so in play consciousness articulates the conditions of human fulfillment. The "long-held presuppositions"—precisely those of the adult world—must be abandoned and another order, based on a totally different logic, created. In play, each day begins with grace, not law. Every night is a moment of forgetting. Man must begin again. The adult world, by the fact that it preserves today what was organized yesterday, never forgets. And it therefore never forgives. It is cruel. As the dinosaur and the dragon proclaim that they cannot afford freedom, so our social organization preserves itself for its own destruction.

The world of play lives by forgetting. The long-held presuppositions never become a law of human behavior. It is possible and necessary to remember the past, but never as in itself a value to be upheld. Man remains the author and director of the script. And the future can be created according to the shape love takes in imagination. It is along these lines, I believe, that we must understand Jesus' admonition that "unless you turn and become like children, you will never enter the kingdom of heaven." Jesus was a debunker, a jester. He was systematically committed to the task of turning the most cherished values of his society upside down. His behavior was much worse than cheating at the official game: he simply refused to play it. Through his words and actions, over and over again he rejected the given rules and proposed new ones. Tradition and law, he indicated, had been converted into a game of human hypocrisy which could not be taken seriously. Accordingly, he did not come to reform or put new wine into old wineskins. His was a different game. Whereas his contemporaries—like our own—were committed to the preservation of the past in the present, he wanted to open the present for the future.

Those who want to preserve the past in the present do it by supporting old values. If the human task, on the contrary, is to prepare the way for the new, then old values have to be broken. Had Jesus been a social reformer he would have been hailed as a religious genius or as a philosopher. But since he was a jester, he was killed as a subversive. There was no mistake in this. The religious and political authorities did not, by a regrettable error, kill a good man. Jesus was dangerous. Although he never used the sword, in and through his language and actions the world as it was seen and sustained by the dominant powers was stripped of its religious ideological garment and thereby reduced to a comic episode. He had to be condemned.

Thus, when he says that we must become like children, he is not praising helplessness. He is inviting us to join the game of freedom and creativity, preconditions of human wholeness and social rebirth. Dance, celebration, and joy, the substance of the heavenly "sabbath"—the day when productivity is forbidden and all is play—are now only hope. They are the material of a utopia. True, as we act we are to embody this hope—to enjoy, express, and celebrate it. But watch out! This is only the "first fruits," the *aperitif* of something still to come. Creation is not yet free. It groans in travail. The dragon is still alive. So enjoyment of the future now has to beget obedience and discipline. The task is not done. The vision of freedom and its celebration in the present cannot exist without political responsibility. We may rejoice that a child is to be born, but there is much pain still before us.

Is play insanity? Obviously, if your judgment of sanity is determined by the dominant system. The values of play require the abolition of the adult world. Can play be dismissed just because it is enacted by the powerless? Only if you call insanity the attempts of a bird to fly with hurt wings. What is insane is not its painful, clumsy efforts to fly, but rather the hand that broke its wings. The truth of play will become history when impotence becomes power, and when that which is now power is reduced to impotence. "Unless you turn and become like children, you will never enter the kingdom of heaven." Unless you give up the dominant logic of this present order of things and become creative, you will not live to see the future. You are doomed to extinction.

7

The Utopian Intention of Imagination

Perhaps future generations will describe our epoch with wonder and amazement as the time when man rediscovered himself as a utopian being—the time when he ceased to be ashamed of his desires and proclaimed to the whole world that he was in love with his dreams and that his visions were for him more important than reality. Until now, he has accepted his social role as if it were his own identity. Who are you? I am a businessman, I am a professor, I am a housewife, I am a garbage collector. I am what I do. But his private diary, written in blood and tears, with grief and joy—his highest thoughts about himself, the book of his hopes—was locked from the world.

Then he discovered that there was more sanity in his vision than in reality. Shame on the realist! Shame on him who accepts the rules of the game! Shame on him who calls the absurdity of the world sanity! And he gained courage to proclaim to the whole world: "I have a dream!" And the heart was then allowed to make its long-repressed confessions of love.

We dream of peace. This is something new, for in the past we have thought victories more important. What we really loved was the death of our enemies. This is the secret hidden under the fanfare of military parades and marches. They are liturgies of death, and the fascination they have exercised over us is an indication of how committed we have been to the worship of death.

We dream of freedom. Our civilization has made us believe that the only things that matter are those that can be bought and sold—that freedom is the thing or the space that can become mine. I am free within the fences marked NO TRESPASSING. I am free when I can choose from five different kinds of dog food. As the fox remarked to the little prince, men "buy things all ready made at the shops. But there is no shop anywhere where one can buy friendship . . ."[1] We are discovering that freedom has more to do with creation than with buying. Mice, too, can learn to choose between five different levers; but only man can give birth to something new. We are learning that freedom is not primarily related to our power over things, whether economic or military, since most of the time the most important things are free. They cannot be bought and sold—only shared.

We dream of pleasure. We are told every day that pleasure is produced by certain institutional gimmicks. We have pleasure when we buy certain things, when we use certain products, when we go to certain places. So in order to feel pleasure or satisfaction one must be properly related to these institutions —which means that one must buy or sell. The pleasure-delivering lever must be pressed. Yet we are discovering that this is not true. The most important things in life cannot be either bought or sold. Joy is free, and pleasure and satisfaction can be found outside our present institutional arrangements.

1. Antoine de Saint–Exupéry, *The Little Prince* (1963), p. 83.

Among our most passionate dreams is the hope that man may rediscover his lost harmony with nature, perhaps because here we are touching the very foundations of our civilization. Our society is built upon the displacement of nature as the basic point of reference for man's life, and the substitution of the world of organization. Freud once belittled the neurotic as a person who lives his desires as "substitute-gratifications" for the real world. We are much worse. Not only do we not live our desires, but we have exchanged the very extension of our bodies —nature—for the impersonal structures of Organization. Our lives are canned in subways, elevators, cement, synthetic food, supermarkets, TVs, offices and, above all, in clocks. A repressed body cannot avoid thinking of its liberation. And it begins to dream of the recovery not only of nature, but of itself. Yes! For it has been lost to man. Organization, discipline, and routine have made us numb and incapable of feeling. Even afraid of feeling. Indeed, it is only by making us numb that Organization suceeds in transforming our body into one of its functions. If it were not so, the body would have rebelled long ago.

One vision follows another. But they are not isolated incidents. They are born of a single emotional matrix which gives them the unity of variations on a given motif. "The whole created universe groans in all its parts as if in the pangs of childbirth" (Rom. 8:22). And what does it long for? Freedom.

There is a sense in which man is never free. For man is relationship. To be alive and conscious is to be permanently involved in a complex network of relationships which are going to condition my being and my behavior. Freedom, in the sense of existing outside these conditions, is an illusion. However, to jump from this conclusion to the other, namely, that man's being and behavior are products of physiological stimuli, is false too. As we have already seen, this is true of animals, but man is able to take these material elements and give them new shape. He can be creative. As far as man is concerned, freedom is the power to take the material conditions of his life and give them form according to his intention.

This is the secret of all the utopian visions men are having today. They proclaim that social organization as a form of repression and control must be abolished and the earth transformed into a place of human recovery. Man is trying desperately to find ways to deal with the earth so that organization results naturally from the growth of life and experience. This was the passionate hope behind the Czech political experiment aborted by the Russian invasion. And this same hope is behind the Black struggle for liberation both abroad and in this country; behind Women's Lib, the Gay Lib, the once active student movements of protest, and an infinite variety of struggles all over the world. It is this hope that becomes poetry and literature in the Soviet Union or protest song wherever life is being repressed, thereby expressing what life itself is saying. Not so much among the professionals of hope, but in the thought and actions of humble Christians who are living the pains of childbirth, hope takes shape.

But at this point we are interrupted. Realism cuts in to inform us with a condescending smile: "Your utopias can be beautiful. But it is not for nothing that they are u-topias—according to the Greek, 'not a place.' Reality has no room for these hopes. Your utopias are unrealizable dreams, in no way different from the madness of magic or the foolishness of play." Reality determines what is possible. The limits of what can be in the future are laid down by what is real now. Nothing that goes beyond these limits can ever exist. As Merton puts it, to try to create social change against the logic of the social system is to be involved in "ritual," in attempting to transform the world by the mere power of ideas, just like the magician. This is, indeed, what utopians seem to try to do. "The utopians attempted to evolve the solution of the social problem out of the human brain," Engels observed. "Society presented nothing but wrongs; to remove these was the task of reason. It was necessary, then, to discover a new and more perfect system of social order and to impose this upon society from without by propaganda. . . ."[2]

So the idea of peace must be dismissed as unrealistic. A social system built upon the logic of war may speak of small wars, big wars, wars of extermination, chemical and bacteriological wars —even the control of war. But one cannot speak of peace. Peace is a utopian dream.

The same is true of freedom. Our rationalized Organization makes room for the most varied discussion of means of control. Shall we condition the mouse by pain or pleasure? Shall we allow him to know that he is being controlled or not? Subliminal techniques or open torture? Different means—one function. But freedom: this the system cannot afford. Freedom is thus declared to be a utopian illusion.

And what about ecology? Our society is based on the ravaging of our resources and the dumping of refuse on our environment. This is how the economy operates. We may speak of when, where, and how to pollute, but to stop pollution is a utopian dream. As Standard Oil advertises, in a mixture of realism and cynicism: WE TAKE SULFUR OUT OF OIL IN VENEZUELA TO KEEP IT OUT OF THE AIR AT HOME.[3]

It is as simple as this: if the present reality is to continue, these hopes can never be realized. There is no possibility of fulfilling them within the limits of our present social organization. When realism declares these dreams to be utopias, it is unwittingly revealing the extremely narrow limits of the reality in whose name it speaks. Utopias are unrealizable not by necessity but by

2. Friedrich Engels, *Socialism, Utopian and Scientific* (n.d.), p. 58.
3. Advertisement in the *Saturday Review*, April 17, 1971.

imposition. It is the game of reality that makes the realization of utopias impossible.

Why do people continue to have utopian dreams, if they know they are impossible? Let me answer by asking, Why is it that *you* go on dreaming if you know your dreams will never come true? But this is the wrong question; dreams are not to be taken as if they were meant to predict the future. Dreams spring from the unconscious dynamics of life, and they both reveal and hide its secrets. Like magic and play, utopias are social dreams. They, too, are born out of the unconscious dynamics of life, no longer in its individual but now in its social form. And as Feuerbach pointed out, "Even in dreams we do not find ourselves in emptiness or in heaven, but on earth, in the realm of reality."[4] Imagination is not an instrument of clairvoyance made for revealing the secrets of the future or of another world. It is a mirror. The impossible it reflects is the impossible that is actually lived. The secret of utopias is thus the reality from which they grow.

Symbols have no significance in themselves. That is to say, they are not self-elucidating. If one wants to know the meaning of symbols, one has to know their history. Who produced them? What fears and hopes, what anxieties and aspirations were mixed in the womb that gave them birth? And why? What is life's purpose underneath the whole process?

The message is not always clear. But neither are our dreams, whether good or bad. Symbols always hide their wisdom under the guise of folly. Jesters, visionaries, clowns, monsters, saying things that are offensive or attractive, gay or terrifying, ridiculous or dreadful, all are combined in our social dreams and nightmares. This has always been true of the deepest longings of the soul. It is easy and natural to express one's desire for a new

4. Ludwig Feuerbach, *The Essence of Christianity* (1957), p. xxxix.

toy, a dress, a car, or a house. Our language has definite ways of expressing these wishes. But when the heart moves beyond the NO TRESPASSING signs which are posted at the very borders of our social order, we discover that we lack means of expression. The desires, the emotions, the hopes are there. But how name them, if they are nameless? Because they are utopian they cannot be referred to in our normal universe of language. And so most of the time the underlying truth of life remains no more than "Inarticulate groans" (Rom. 8:26).

Can we dismiss utopias as if they were products of a neurotic mind? This is what Freud did with religion, magic, and play. No —in order to be true to Freud himself we must apply to utopias the same criteria that he applied to dreams. And as we analyze the story of their genesis we discover that they spring from very specific forms of social life. As Mannheim has pointed out, "The key to the intelligibility of utopias is the structural situation of that social stratum which at any given time espouses them. The substance and form of the utopia does not take place in a realm which is independent of social life."[5]

Thus, just as it is impossible to stop a human being from dreaming, so it is impossible to prevent certain social groups from being utopian. It was Durkheim who called our attention to this fact. "Does someone think of a perfect society, where justice and truth would reign sovereign, and from which evil in all its forms would be banished for ever? But this society is not an empirical fact, definite and observable; it is a fancy, a dream with which men have lightened their sufferings, but in which they never really lived." Where does this vision come from? From a sick mind? No. It is "a natural product of social life. When some oppose the ideal society to the real society [as falsity to truth and illusion to reality, as the ideologues of realism have

5. Karl Mannheim, *Ideology and Utopia* (1936), pp. 185, 187.

done] like two antagonists which would lead us in opposite directions, they materialize and oppose abstractions. The ideal society is not outside of the real society; it is part of it."[6] To dispose of utopias as irrational products of consciousness is to refuse to hear the voice of life itself. Because, as Tillich once remarked, "utopias participate in truth. To deny them is thus a dangerous artifice, because in this negation one would be simply overcoming the truth that they hide."[7]

I once had a long conversation with a man who considered himself a committed Christian, about the shocking contradictions between the standards of life and the values of typical middle-class persons in this country and the prevailing conditions of life among the poor nations of the world. I had the impression that we were about to reach some interesting conclusions, since we had agreed that affluence is to a great degree a result of the exploitation of the poor by the rich nations of the world, and poverty, in turn, the product of an economy which only operates along the logic of profit and greed. Suddenly our conversation came to a halt and he made this candid but at the same time frightful confession: "I understand what you mean. I am able to see the absurdity of the situation. But look: I have a nice house, a summer house, two cars, and a boat. I can see, but I can't feel. So no matter how hard I try, I will remain committed to the values of this life which is so good for me."

It reminded me of what the Bible says about the rich and powerful: how hard is it for them to enter the Kingdom of God. The possibility is not closed. But only as an exception, as a miracle, as a possibility which does not belong to us. The rich and powerful have no choice: their own existential conditions

6. Émile Durkheim, *The Elementary Forms of the Religious Life* (1969), pp. 467–69.

7. Quoted by Pierre Furter, *L'Imagination Créatrice, la Violence et le Changement Social* (1968), p. 3/3. (My translation.)

determine that they must be committed to the preservation of things as they are. Reality is friendly to them—how could it be otherwise, if they are the ones who have built it up by means of their economic, military, and scientific power? History does not tell us of a single case in which the powerful have given up power willingly. Their hearts are no longer restless. The present fulfills their yearnings, and this very fact creates for them the impossibility of transcendence. Their minds cannot go beyond it. The ultimate maxim of their behavior is that "facts are values." Therefore they must be preserved. And because their hearts are set on the given and on the present, they must abolish imagination. They have no choice; their power and wealth force them to be realists. Obviously the present order of things delivers pleasure. Obviously they find in it a sense of security. They have built what Augustine called a "private form of good": an order which is totally for them. It has a beauty of its own—provided you are one of the wealthy and powerful. It has a goodness of its own—provided we look at it with the eyes of someone who is in control. A special morality emerges. The good and the true are defined so as to validate the status quo. It was the understanding of this fact that led Nietzsche to exclaim: "O my brothers, who represents the greatest danger for all of man's future? Is it not the good and the just? Inasmuch as they say and feel in their hearts, 'We already know what is good and just, and we have it too; woe unto those who still seek here.' "[8]

Just like the mice: they have the monopoly of the pleasure-delivering lever. The status quo becomes their highest good, and ultimately their god. This is where futurology is born: science serving to preserve the rules of the present into the future—knowledge which proclaims that the only possible fu-

8. Friedrich Nietzsche, *Thus Spoke Zarathustra*, in Walter Kaufmann, ed., *The Portable Nietzsche* (1968), p. 324.

ture is that defined by the principle of limited possibilities. The more things change, the more they are to remain the same.

This is the reason why pleasure and well-being always generate a conservative posture. If Bultmann is correct in his definition of sin as fear of the future and the desperate attempt to forestall its coming, then the dominant classes are always involved in sin whether they like it or not, whether they have "good intentions" or not. Indeed, one of the ironies of the situation is that the good intentions of the privileged classes are always controlled by the ultimate value that things must remain the same. " 'Stability,' insisted the Controller, 'stability. The primal and ultimate need. Stability.' " See how inextricably intertwined well-being, power, the desire to control, and realism are. Where your treasure is, there must your heart be also. And if your heart has elected the present order of things as its ultimate good, your mind will have to be "adapted to the pattern of this present world." As I remarked in the beginning, pleasure is the mother of idolatry, because "where there are oases there are also idols."[9]

Nobody likes pain. But without the ability to feel it one's body is in danger. Pain is at the service of life. It is an alarm system which informs our organism that something is wrong. If you touch a hot surface the reaction is immediate. The body does not even bother to interpret; what causes pain must be avoided. If you had not felt it, you would have left your hand on the burning surface without knowing that your body tissues were being destroyed.

Society is an extension of our body. If some of its members are feeling pain, this is a warning signal that something is wrong. But the classes in power have lost the ability to feel it. As happens with all those who are intoxicated with their own satisfac-

9. *Ibid.*, p. 215.

tions, they nod approvingly when their false prophets proclaim: "All is well."

Vision is born out of pain. As Buber pointed out, "All suffering under a social order that is senseless prepares the soul for vision."[10] This is not the suffering that is the unavoidable consequence of the fact that we are bodies (I may fall ill, my wife may be killed in an accident, my son might be crippled by an incurable disease). All living beings are subject to the chances of life —animals, oppressed, and oppressors alike. But I am concerned now with the kind of suffering that is the result of a social organization based on inequality—that depends on the division between those who wield power and those upon whom it is used. The weak nations of the world, ethnic minorities, women, children, elderly people, persons who cannot achieve in academic or professional fields according to the standards of those who control the game: these are the members of the social body who feel the pain and therefore the absurdity of reality.

It is rather significant that for the Bible reality is not to be measured by its highest accomplishments but rather by the fact that it makes God suffer. It names God "the suffering Servant." Where is He to be found? Wherever man is suffering. "When I was hungry you gave me nothing to eat, when thirsty nothing to drink; when I was a stranger you gave me no home, when naked you did not clothe me; when I was ill and in prison you did not come to my help. . . . Anything you did not do for one of these, however humble, you did not do for me" (Matt. 25: 43–45). This may sound rather strange, but what the biblical symbols clearly indicate is that the body of God, the body of the Liberator, is the body of the oppressed and dispossessed. And it is from this solidarity in suffering that the future is imagined. Because it is engendered amid suffering, it implies the abolition

10. Martin Buber, *Paths in Utopia* (1958), p. 7.

of the conditions of power that have created suffering. "How blest are the sorrowful; they shall find consolation. . . . How blest are those who hunger and thirst to see right prevail; they shall be satisfied. . . . How blest are those who have suffered persecution for the cause of right; the kingdom of Heaven is theirs" (Matt. 5:4, 6, 10).

This is magic. The logic of reality is abolished. The principle of limited possibilities is denied, and the future reverses the logic of the present.

Mice learn that they can avoid shocks on one side of their box by jumping over the partition that divides it. Thus the problem is solved by a spatial movement away from pain-producing zones toward those that give pleasure. The spatial organization remains the same. What changes is one's location in it. Society is in many ways similar to that box. Just by looking at the map of a city one can identify the zones of pain and those of comfort. Check the real-estate section of a newspaper. The price of a house in the area you have your eye on will tell you whether it is a "nice neighborhood" or not. Aside from the geographical division of the human world into zones of pain and pleasure, we have the same thing in the class structure. Certain groups are destined to work more, suffer more, earn less, die sooner, and endure discrimination. Others work less, earn more, have more pleasure, have a better chance of living longer, and enjoy prestige and status.

Just as mice were conditioned to avoid pain by changing their location, so society conditions us to believe that our problems will be solved if we can jump the partition. The affluent classes are those who have succeeded. But if the others only try hard enough, they will join the club. The point is not to try to keep up with the Joneses, but to *be* the Joneses. One assumes that the organization of our space cannot be changed, and does not need to be. It is all right. It is we who must learn to jump higher. We must move to the pleasure-delivering areas. If we cannot man-age it, at least we can prepare the way for our children. We must give them good educations so that they will get white-collar jobs. It is common to speak of vertical social mobility. This is a rather accurate description of the situation. The lower the class level, the greater the incidence of pain. The higher the level, the greater the incidence of pleasure. This is why the ideal of the normal man is to go "up" in life.

For a long period in their history, this is what Blacks tried to do. If Whites have a monopoly of the pleasure-producing de-vices of society, it is necessary to be on good terms with them. Blacks tried to be recognized as clean, hardworking, orderly people. They wanted the Whites to know that though they had black skins, their souls were white. By behaving in this way they might even be rewarded. The magic door in the cage might be opened, and they would be allowed into the world of pleasure. This was the philosophy of integration. Women did the same thing. They knew that they were pleasure-delivering gadgets and that by skillfully playing the game of men, they could enjoy security and status—pleasures which are the monopoly of males.

The nations of the Third World, in turn, were not in any way different from the mice. They were locked into poverty and underdevelopment. And just on the other side of the box, what did they see? A society of waste and pleasure. They tried hard to jump the partition, but soon learned that unless they were on good terms with the Masters, they could not do it. As John Foster Dulles once put it, there are definite advantages in being friendly toward the United States and definite disadvantages in not being friendly. But we live in a world in which nothing is gratuitous. The price of economic help was political allegiance. "All this I will give you," they were told, "if only you will fall down and pay me homage." Because power has a monopoly on earthly pleasures and satisfactions, it is only by submitting to its conditions that one can attain them. The right lever must be pressed. Jump, mice, jump!

The game is complete. Nothing is lacking. Read the instructions carefully. Use the right ingredients. Press the right buttons. The end-product will be the pleasure pie. If you do not succeed, try harder.

A few manage to join the Joneses' club. But the geography of pain and pleasure remains the same. The petty triumphs of the individual are no sign of hope to those who remain entrapped. They simply indicate that the monopoly has admitted another associate director. Little by little a few begin to suspect that the dice are loaded. And suddenly a new insight changes one's whole outlook: the issue is not to win the game, but to change its regulations. Utopian vision is born. And imagination spreads its wings and carries us to another land, where life is played under different rules. Little by little the unconscious groaning becomes articulate speech, and the original suspicion becomes open denunciation. Like the magician, the heart begins to "name the things that are absent."[11] It "summons things that are not yet in existence as if they already were." And this is a true act of exorcism. The spell of the existing order of things is broken, and man is free "from the massive presence of the immediate present."[12] He can now envisage the future as a possible task, something that can be created according to the intentions of the heart.

This implies a revolution in man's behavior, because right here freedom is born. Man begins to act out of his love for the future, a future which nowhere exists as a physiological or material stimulus. "Let the future and the farthest be for you the cause of your today," Zarathustra cried out. And as you live

11. Paul Valéry, "Poésie et Pensée Abstraite," in *Oeuvres* (1957), I, 1327.
12. Furter, *op. cit.*, p. 3/7. My translation.

your now, "walk among men as among the fragments of the future."[13]

The present must be made pregnant. The creative intention must take shape within its womb, "so that the present itself is given a form which makes possible the eruption of the future."[14] What am I to do? Midwifery. Creation groans in travail. Already there is a new life in its womb—the source of our hope. As J. Révai put it, tactics is nothing more than the future appearing as present.[15] So one lives literally by the power of something one does not see. "For we have been saved, though only in hope," remarks Paul. "Now to see is no longer to hope. . . ." (Rom. 8:24).

The utopian vision liberates man from the determinism of material forces which create the compulsion of avoidance behavior, and definitely says No to any solution of the problem of suffering in terms of successive dislocations and relocations within the existing geography of pain and pleasure. Once in love with his vision, the question for man is no longer to avoid pain or the satisfactions we are calling pleasure, but to create a new world. And a fascinating thing happens: for the sake of his creative object, man is even able to conquer suffering. In the words of Paul, hope produces endurance. If the way to a new future goes through pain, man takes up risk and death joyfully.

How can we account for Socrates and Jesus, the prophets and the revolutionaries, the moving procession of forgotten martyrs who suffered or died for the sake of a vision—Bonhoeffer and Berrigan, Gandhi and Martin Luther King? "Others were tortured to death. . . . Others, again, had to face jeers and flogging, even fetters and prison bars. They were stoned, they were sawn in two, they were put to the sword, they went about dressed in

13. Nietzsche, *op. cit.*, pp. 174, 251.
14. Pierre Furter, *Educação e Vida* (1968), p. 61. My translation.
15. Quoted by Mannheim, *op. cit.*, p. 221 *n.*

skins of sheep or goats, in poverty, distress, and misery. . . . They were refugees in deserts and on the hills, hiding in caves and holes in the ground. . . . and yet they did not enter upon the promised inheritance. . . ." (Heb. 11:35–40). Physical pain and pleasure lose their finality. They are overcome, and man discovers his freedom in the act of bringing a new earth into being.

What is the hidden secret of this dream of the human mind? It reveals that man has not given up hope. He still claims the future for himself. Reality can only produce a shocking future, it cannot be otherwise. How should a wild vine bear sweet grapes? No, the future can be friendly, it can bring joy—provided man has the vision and courage to create it; provided he stubbornly refuses to accept it as an unavoidable, rigidly determined fact which is already snowballing in his direction. Here is the fundamental difference between the language of futurology and that of prophecy. Futurology wants to describe how the future will be. It remains strictly within the limits of the reality principle. Prophecy and utopia, on the contrary, see the future as a task. They want to "make room for the possible, as opposed to a passive acquiescence in the present actual state of affairs. It is symbolic thought which overcomes the natural inertia of man and endows him with a new ability, the ability constantly to reshape his human universe. The future of which the prophets spoke was not an empirical fact but an ethical and religious task. Their ideal future signifies the negation of the empirical world, the 'end of all days.' But it contains at the same time the hope and the assurance of a 'new heaven and a new earth.' "[16] Here man is affirming that the living and not the dead are in charge—the dead who are with us through the present they have bequeathed to us. And if life is in charge, one may still hope.

16. Ernst Cassirer, *An Essay on Man* (1953), pp. 86, 78–79.

In utopias we see the logic of creativity reaching its final limit. Long-held presuppositions must be given up. Only then can the new world begin. Nowhere is this so beautifully portrayed as in the biblical myths of creation. Myths of the beginning are actually a projected way of talking about the future one envisages. They are attempts to establish in the past, foundations for hopes of the future. They are dreams in which what is hoped for appears in the past tense. One must change the tense of the verb if one is to discover their meaning.

There is the primeval situation! The objective reality is darkness and water, an amorphous raw material entrapped in its own disorder and lack of purpose. Chaos. Out of it, by itself, neither life nor order nor beauty can emerge. Chaos can be transcended only if its irrationality is overcome. But then a magic operation begins. Intention becomes deed: the word is pronounced. The heart reveals its longings, and a miracle occurs. Why miracle? Because the new thing cannot be explained as having been *caused* by chaos. There is no logical nexus between them, no continuing likeness. The old things have passed away. Behold, everything is new.

When reality is trapped in its own irrationality, it is exactly like the primeval chaos. Its creative possibilities are exhausted. The Spirit must reshape it anew. Now order is created. Light appears. Intention *in-forms* reality. It negates the reality principle and conquers it by the pleasure principle. Beauty, goodness, and joy become part of the world. "And God saw that it was good." The symphony goes on. The same motif is taken up again and repeated with variations until it reaches its climax. Creation is finished. Intention has triumphed over chaos and darkness. And then the Creator rests. It is no longer time to create, but time to enjoy. Beyond the creative moment, the moment of play.

It is very easy to dismiss utopias as unrealizable dreams.

> Then the wolf shall live with the sheep,
>   and the leopard lie down with the kid;
> the calf and the young lion shall grow up together,
>   and a little child shall lead them;
>   the cow and the bear shall be friends,
>   and their young shall lie down together.
> The lion shall eat straw like cattle;
> the infant shall play over the hole of the cobra
> and the young child dance over the viper's nest.
> They shall not hurt or destroy in all my holy mountain;
>   for as the waters fill the sea,
> so shall the land be filled with the knowledge of the Lord.
> [Isa. 11:6–9]

> They shall beat their swords into mattocks
>   and their spears into pruning-knives;
> nation shall not lift sword against nation
>   nor ever again be trained for war. [Isa. 2:4]

Is this a blueprint of the future, a primitive futurologic effort? Obviously not. The heart is revealing the conditions of human happiness. As in the myth of creation, everything is very good. The logic of desire has triumphed over the power of reality. Death, suffering, injustice, chaos are conquered. The old order of life is brought to an end, so that life itself is resurrected and preserved in a new body. Man is reconciled with reality—but not by giving up his desires and becoming a realist, but rather by giving power to his hopes in order to perform the magical operation. This is why in the biblical symbols the Suffering Servant, in whom the desire for salvation is born, becomes the Messiah, the power that dissolves the old and creates the new. The hidden secret of the utopian vision is that man will remain restless and unhappy until the day when his hopes triumph over facts. And implicit in this hope is the conviction that desire must be given power to defeat the powers that conspire against life.

I hope implies *I will.* And *I will* is always will to power.

It is rather significant, as Mannheim points out, that "it is always the dominant group which is in full accord with the existing order that determines what is to be regarded as utopian."[17] In other words, that group determines what is generally accepted as possible or impossible. But the criteria of possibility are relative. It is impossible for man to live under water. For fish, however, the impossible thing is to live out of it. Possibility and impossibility are relative to the structures that declare them. When a system affirms something to be impossible, it is simply disclosing its own limits. To say that a vision is utopian reveals almost nothing about the vision itself, but definitely unveils the logic of the system that passes this judgment. And since the vision emerges from the very experience of the absurdity of the system, by declaring it to be utopian the system unwittingly confesses the need for its own extinction.

Utopias are born when life discovers that its body is doomed to death. And because life wants to live, it has to say No to its own body. It has to elaborate a project of metamorphosis; the caterpillar must become a butterfly. But for this to happen the caterpillar has to disappear. The problem is that no dying nation, no dying order or institution or civilization will accept its fate. This is why utopians and prophets are dismissed as heretics, subversive or insane. The tragedy of utopia is the tragedy of the cross. The creators are put to death because of their vision.

O my brothers, one man once saw into the hearts of the good and the just and said, "They are pharisees." But he was not understood. The good and the just themselves were not permitted to understand him: their spirit is imprisoned in their good conscience. The stupidity of the good is unfathomably shrewd. This, however, is the truth: the *good*

17. Mannheim, *op. cit.,* p. 183.

must be pharisees—they have no choice. The good *must* crucify him who invents his own virtue.[18]

But even in this tragedy, there is promise and hope. Men are still willing to die for their visions. And their suffering and death will be the seed from which a resurrected future emerges.

18. Nietzsche, *op. cit.*, p. 324.

8

Imagination Made Flesh: Personality

In our civilization magic rituals, play, and utopian dreams are considered symptoms of sickness. The reason is very simple. We define sanity as behavior which is functional, and we equate mental health with pragmatism and realism. And it so happens that neither magic, play, nor utopias pass the test.

But let me ask, is there any ultimate reason to go on assuming that the logic of our society should be the criterion for determining when life is sane or insane? Is life itself to be judged by the way it fits into the social system? Is life nothing more than a function of the structures of our social organization? What is the ultimate point of reference for our understanding of sanity and what is deranged?

This question can be answered by means of another. Who is the creator, society or man? What is the creation, man or society? The creator is always the ultimate point of reference for understanding his creation. No painting, no song, no poem has meaning in itself, independent of the intention behind the act of composition. Society is to man what the work of art is to the artist. Our institutions, structures, and culture have been created. They follow man's intentions, they are products of his hands. They were meant to be extensions of his body and of his heart, instruments for survival and means of expression. In the logic of life, life itself is the only absolute. It is the ultimate criterion by which all it has created must be judged. It is not for society, therefore, to define what form of life is sane or insane. On the contrary, it is for life to say whether indeed society is sane or not.

The conditions of our birth tend to hide this element of appropriateness from us. When we enter our world, we find it already there, ready and solid, old and strong. Before we are, it has already been. Because we were not on hand as it was progressively created, we come to believe mistakenly that society is the creator and man the creation. We are educated for reality: that is, we are made to believe that human wholeness depends on our ability to fit into the social scheme. Life has become a function of something else beside itself, a means to an alien end.

Once thus conditioned, consciousness cannot imagine freedom as an actuality, or envisage the possibility of repeating the creative act. What is happening here, however, is that man allows his life to be defined by institutional programs brought into being by people who are now gone. Through institutions, the hands and brains of the dead continue to live among us and shape our present. When we permit the logic of our social system to be the ultimate criterion for the dividing line between sanity and insanity, we are in fact allowing our identity to be defined by the dead.

The consequence of this amnesia as to the origins of our world are fateful. Life becomes trapped in the mistakes of past generations and is prevented from making new creative syntheses.

The logic of the dinosaur triumphs, and man loses his vision of the possibility of a new beginning.

Now, what are magic, play, and utopian dreams?

They are the many voices of life speaking about the conditions of its survival and expression. They are liturgies the heart creates and enacts in order to keep alive the hope that life will be able to overthrow the defining power of reality.

They are man's multiple languages, through which he articulates his unconscious groanings and protests against being transformed into a function and a means. In imagination he speaks of himself as the ultimate end and sole criterion of sanity—and this is why it is dismissed as unsound. It defines what human wholeness is, in a way that the prevailing rules of sanity themselves prohibit.

Thus magic rituals, play, and utopian dreams are not unfortunate accidents in the development of man. They are expressions of the deepest aspirations of the human soul. This is what Malinowski discovered in his analysis of magic. He never asked the pragmatic question: "Is magic an adequate technology?" If he had, he would have imposed upon it the hidden assumptions of our social order. His were different questions: "Where does it come from? What are the vital elements that lead man to create it?" And his conclusion was that magic was the result of a "universal psycho-physiological mechanism"[1] peculiar to man. It is an expression of life itself. Huizinga was moved to a similar conclusion in his study of play. In play, he remarked (as we have seen), "we have to do with an absolutely primary category of life" which, far from being accidental or superfluous, is the foundation and beginning of the human world.[2]

What shall we say about utopias? Are they illusions of a sick mind? "These aspirations have their roots in us," says Durk-

1. Bronislaw Malinowski, *Magic, Science or Religion* (1948), p. 80.
2. Johan Huizinga, *Homo Ludens* (1955), p. 3.

heim. "They come from the very depth of our beings."[3] Tillich arrived at the same conclusion. Utopias "must have a foundation in the structure of man himself," he pointed out. "For in the last analysis only that has significance which has a foundation in the structure of man."[4] The general conclusion I am driving at has been stated with unsurpassed simplicity and clarity by Berger and Luckmann.

The origins of a symbolic universe have their roots in the constitution of man. If man in society is a world-constructor, this is made possible by his constitutionally given world-openness, which already implies the conflict between order and chaos. Human existence is, *ab initio*, an ongoing externalization. As man externalizes himself he constructs the world into which he externalizes himself. In the process of externalization, he projects his own meaning into reality. Symbolic universes, which proclaim that *all* reality is humanly meaningful and call upon the entire cosmos to signify the validity of human existence, constitute the farthest reaches of this projection.[5]

What does it mean to say that man is open to the world? It means that his conscious life is not a mere duplication of what is objectively out there. That is true for animals. Man, however, is not a realist but a world constructor. What he is given is, for him, simply the raw material for a task still to be carried out.

And he creates. His model? Himself. His world is the externalization of his values and aspirations, the incarnation of his intention, the objectifying of the spirit.

This means that for man his eyes are not a simple duplicating device. He sees with his heart. He looks at reality, not under pressure of its mere factualness but perceiving the avenues of

3. Emile Durkheim, *The Elementary Forms of the Religious Life* (1969), p. 468.
4. Paul Tillich, *Political Expectation* (1971), p. 125.
5. Peter Berger and Thomas Luckmann, *The Social Construction of Reality* (1967), p. 104.

its possibilities. Reality itself does not reveal the secret of what is possible. Indeed, it does not know anything about this—just as the block of marble does not know what it may become as the intention of the artist gives it shape. It is the aspirations and longings of man that draw out the secrets of the possible.

To see with the heart is not an abnormality, unless of course we are willing to dismiss life itself as such. The very constitution of man establishes this life program. "These are the conditions of wholeness and sanity," imagination proclaims. "The world must be an expression of man's values." When there is harmony between values and the world, man feels that he lives in a meaningful universe—even if it is not quantitatively rich. On the other hand, if this harmony is threatened and he feels overwhelmingly that his values are being destroyed by reality, then his personality disintegrates even if his world is affluent and he himself materially wealthy. "It is the human ego that carries the search for a world to love: or rather this project, in the unconscious stratum of the ego, guides human consciousness in the restless search for an object that can satisfy its love."[6] All forms of life that existed before man have accepted reality as being all right. This is why they have never tried to transform it. They did not create culture, and they survived only by adapting. Man is the only being who refuses to accept reality as it is. This is the uniqueness of human consciousness. As Feuerbach put it, "The brute has only a simple, man a twofold life: in the brute, the inner life is one with the outer; man has both an inner and an outer life."[7] Animals duplicate the world inside themselves. Even when they suffer they never *question* reality. This is how things are, and if it is to survive the animal must learn how to play the game. The possibility that things could be different from what they are never enters its consciousness. Man's con-

6. Norman O. Brown, *Life Against Death* (1959), p. 46.
7. Ludwig Feuerbach, *The Essence of Christianity* (1957), p. 2.

sciousness, however, is split. He is able to see what exists. But at the same time he senses that there are things lacking, while some present things ought not to be there. His imagination explores a hidden world of the possible, and hope is born in him that such a world can be created through his intention. And he falls in love with this dream. This is what keeps coming back and invading the sphere of reality through magic, play, utopian dreams, and the manifold expressions of imagination, all repeating the secret of man's life program: Reality is not informed by my desires; but it should be. This is what personality is all about.

Personality emerges in the first act of negation. When, for the first time, the suspicion appears that the world is not as it ought to be, man is born. This is an act of rebellion. It indicates a qualitative change. Life has succeeded in creating a new logic for itself. From then on it will not survive solely by adapting to the real. For the real will be transfigured by life: it will be organized according to man's desires and become a mirror of his values. What constitutes the human ego is a primordial negative act which, even before it takes form in real action, is already present in the structure of consciousness. Rebellion is not one among many different moods man may eventually have; it is rather the distinctive element that separates him from animals and the most fundamental presupposition on which his whole mental life is based. As Camus put it, "With rebellion, awareness is born."[8]

How offended we are by this word *rebellion!* Who is the rebel? In our minds his face takes shape little by little: eyes full of hatred, heart bursting with resentment, a voice that announces the end and welcomes chaos, hands ready to destroy our most cherished values. How could a loving heart rebel? We associate love with fear of resisting, and kindness with the will-

8. Albert Camus, *The Rebel* (1956), p. 15.

ingness to swallow everything. Behind our stereotyped smiles lurks the apprehension that we might be taken as someone who has the audacity to say No—to resist and to offend. It is true that in many of our ways we pretend to be revolutionaries. But deep inside ourselves we are worshipers of Norman Vincent Peale. How can a friendly, sociable, nice person say anything but Yes?

But we forget that rebellion is the presupposition of any creative act. In planting a garden we rebel against the barrenness of nature. In struggling against disease we rebel against suffering. We speak a word of compassion because we rebel against tears. We fall in love because we rebel against isolation. We are willing to be persecuted for the cause of right because we rebel against oppression and injustice. Animals cannot rebel. This is why they cannot be creative, either. Only one who says No to things as they are is willing to suffer for the creation of the new. The world of culture would be unthinkable apart from the acts of rebellion of those who built it.

What I am saying may sound very odd, since psychoanalysis has been telling us that the source of neurosis is our rebellion against reality. The sick person is one who resists the facts of life and tries to abolish them. Normality is acquiescence to the real; adaptation, adjustment. The ideal of psychoanalytic theory is the abolition of the split that divides consciousness and separates man from the animals, so that he may be content again. As Norman O. Brown puts it, "The way out of neurosis [is] the simple health that animals enjoy, but not man."[9] The split between facts and values is to be dissolved. Facts are to become values, and thus man will become reconciled to the world as it is.

The drawback of this recipe is that it solves the tensions of personality by abolishing personality itself. Prescott Lecky re-

9. Brown, *op. cit.*, p. 311. Cf. p. 19 also.

marks that resistance is not a symptom of illness but rather the
only mechanism by means of which personality holds itself together. Indeed, what is it that constitutes personality? It is a
structure of values. Values are not facts; they are nowhere to be
found in the world out there. Instead of speaking of values we
should rather use the word *valuation*, which indicates that
value is relationship, that it only exists when it is *given* by man.
Now, our values do not fall from the blue. They are engendered
by life itself. They are the body's highest ideas about itself, its
life program, the revelation of its hidden intention to transform
the whole world into an extension of itself. "The nucleus of our
life system, around which the rest of the system revolves, is the
individual's valuation of himself. The individual sees the world
from his own view point, with himself as the center."[10]

However, the world as such is unfriendly. We love our bodies,
we love life, we love our beloved ones. But we see that we are
getting older and that life is coming to an end. We love peace,
justice, play, and freedom. But we see that these values are daily
denied by our society. Freud's advice was that we should stoi-
cally accept things as they are. Yet this would imply the very
dissolution of personality. This is why man builds symbolic universes. Magic, religion, play, art, utopias, ideologies—all are
tools that personality creates to carry on its resistance. When
resistance disappears, personality disappears, and with it the
possibility of the creative act. If one believed the facts of reality
to be values, how could one dare to think of the creation of new
ones? When we see the rebel who resists and says No to reality
—whether by suffering in silence, by singing, by creating religious dreams, by dropping out, by destroying—it is likely that
we will hear the verdict society passes upon him: misfit—insane,
neurotic, heretic.

10. Prescott Lecky, *Self-Consistency: A Theory of Personality* (1961), p. 109.

But do not believe! What is actually happening is that personality is affirming the priority of its values against the brute factualness of a world that conspires against the aspirations of the heart. It is not for society to say what forms of life are sane or insane. Life itself must say whether society is sane or not. And if life finds that society conspires against it, there is no course of action left but resistance and rebellion.

It is obvious that no system will accept the claims of personality, which wants to define the social order in a way the social order itself prohibits. Every social system aspires to say what is right and wrong. In the power to define lies the power to control. As Humpty Dumpty shrewdly observes, if you have power you have the last word. And if you have the last word, you determine how the game of life is to be played. From childhood up we have been told who are the bad guys and who are the good guys. Heroes always wear the badge of law and order; they are at the service of the dominant order of things. The sheriff, the soldier who dies for the flag, the civilian who works for the establishment: these are the heroes who have a place in the national pantheon. For all practical purposes, rather dead than red. Any form of life that contradicts one's definitions does not deserve to exist.

One of the functions of history writing and telling is to define who are the good and who the bad guys. If winners had been losers, history would have been written in a quite different way. Many present national heroes would be found in the gallery of criminals, and vice versa. This is why the winners never allow the losers to become historians. Of necessity, their interpretation of events must be a willful distortion of "what actually took place." Historical monuments, of course, are always erected by the winners. This reflects their determining role in the writing of history, and their consequent power to define what sanity and insanity are.

The Bible has the peculiarity of having been written by those who experienced weakness and defeat, i.e., a community which *of necessity* had to be opposed to the triumphant definitions of power and—derivatively—of what was sane or perverted and unsound. The result is quite disturbing. The Bible turns the normal plot upside down. Villains become heroes and heroes become villains.

I was once told that the children and grandchildren of immigrants who came to this country in great poverty often want to move their deceased ancestors from their graves in the poorer sections of cemeteries to more elegant ones. By this means they hope to reverse the plot and force the dead to tell a story which does not embarrass the living. This is what the Church has done with the Bible. She has unburied characters originally found in the shameful section reserved for villains, and moved them to a nice neighborhood where the bones of respectful, law-abiding, normal people rest. The Church is a skillful undertaker, a clever storyteller. Symbols have been transformed into their opposite. Rebels have become tame. The gospel has become the handmaid of social normality. It could not be otherwise. When the Church ceases to be an oppressed people, and therefore a rebel, she has to assume the role of definer of the situation. The Bible has been incorporated into the historiography of the powerful, in order to add the verdict of the past to the realities of the present. We are made to read it as if it simply confirmed the "normality" in which we live. A certain lady once told me frankly, "The sources of my spiritual life are the Bible and the *Reader's Digest.*"

But the Bible itself, candidly looked at, reverses the definition of what is and is not sane. "God has made the wisdom of this world look foolish," and what the gospel proclaims as wisdom, from the point of view of the existing order "is sheer folly" (1 Cor. 1:18–21).

Jesus was a master in the art of subverting the rules of sanity and insanity. Take, for instance, the parable of the Prodigal Son. By the standards of any respectable social order there cannot be any doubt that he was an irresponsible fellow. His behavior was not mature. He was a dreamer who paid no attention to the rules of the game of life. His brother, on the contrary, was a paradigm of hard work and discipline. But Jesus inverts their roles. The younger brother appears as the one for whom humanity is to be found, whereas the older is symbolic of inhumanity. The same plot is found in the parable of the Good Samaritan. The good guys, the priest and the Levite, play the roles of villains, whereas the bad guy, the Samaritan, is the hero. When Jesus told the chief priests and the elders of the nation —i.e., those who had the monopoly of the definition of normality—that "tax-gatherers and prostitutes are entering the kingdom of God ahead of you" (Matt. 21:31), he simply indicated which social groups had the conditions to understand what he was talking about. Jesus was extremely clear on this point, and there was no possibility of misunderstanding him. This is why he was declared insane; or worse, possessed by a demon. And this explains, further, the reason for Jesus' total despair as to the possibility of "normal" people's ever understanding him, so that he quoted the prophecy of Isaiah: "You may hear and hear, but you will never understand; you may look and look, but you will never see" (Matt. 13:14). The oppressed—yes, they can perceive the absurdity of reality. Their existential condition is what creates the need and possibility of rebellion. The powerful cannot rebel. They can afford to be realists.

There is something somber in all this, for resistance implies the giving up of our most cherished personal hopes. We all dream of buying a nice piece of land, where we will build our house. We want to organize our little space and time in such a way as to feel the world is friendly toward us. How we envy the old trees, their roots going deep inside the earth, solid and sure, proud amidst the storm, friendly when nature is at rest! Now we rebel. Why? Because we have discovered that our world is not as friendly as we expected. Its waters have a bitter taste. Its air smells of decay. How can we enjoy the song of the wind, of the birds and the flowing brooks, if the groaning of men, women, and children fills the space and time in which we live? Only those who close their eyes and ears—only those who have become insensitive—can feel at home in the world as it is. Because we see and hear, we have to say, "I do not belong here." Man discovers that he suffers from an incurable disease, which will follow him wherever he goes: homelessness. He is an exile in the world.

Mozart exerts a strange fascination upon me, perhaps because his sonatas are the aesthetic expression of what I would like my life to be. So simple. A motif is presented; it develops, changes, and is recovered again. Everything makes sense. And then, in no more than twenty minutes, it ends. Nothing abrupt. The close is welcome because it is an act of fulfillment. Everything there was to say has been said. When it began, it was already clear how it was going to unfold and end. But there is always a feeling of sadness when one hears these works. For exiles cannot hope that their lives will be like Mozart's sonatas. They will never find a home; their lives will never be the unfolding of a unified motif. Homelessness and fragmentation go together. One is homeless—forever.

This is one of Nietzsche's dearest themes. Not as tragedy, but as the very essence of what it means to be human. "Exiles shall you be from all father- and forefather-lands," says Zarathustra to his disciples. But is not this the most central theme of the Bible itself? "By faith Abraham obeyed the call to go out to a land destined for himself and his heirs, and left home without knowing where he was to go." The strange fact, however, is that when he arrived at what seemed to be his destination, he went on living as if he did not belong there. "He settled as an alien" —homeless even in the land promised him. He went on "living in tents. . . . For he was looking forward. . . ." (Heb. 11:8–10).

Faith and homelessness belong together. Faith is homelessness. And then we are told that this is what saved him. Strange as it may appear, the Bible understands that man becomes whole and free only after his roots are cut off and he is an exile. There is no way out. If we are not already blind, if we are still able to understand and feel, how can we avoid the conclusion that the present order of things is absurd? From this point on one lives from one's passion for the absent. Out of this tension, the prophet is born.

Thus suffering is not accidental to personality. It belongs to its very essence. It is an indication that we are in touch with the world, a sign both of our presence and of our rebellion—of our being in the world without being domesticated by it. Dostoevsky once remarked that he was sure that "man would never renounce suffering because, after all, suffering is the sole origin of consciousness."[11] This is very difficult for us to understand. We lack what Unamuno called the tragic sense of life: that is, we have not yet realized that it is not possible for freedom and happiness to go together. Freedom is creativity. How can the happy create? By the very fact that they are content they must be committed to the preservation of things as they are. Creativity is born out of an infinite loathing for what makes man suffer. How can one create if one does not know what suffering is? "In a certain sense personality is suffering," remarks Berdyaev. "The struggle to achieve personality presupposes resistance, it demands a conflict with the enslaving power of the world, a refusal to conform to the world. Pain in the human

11. Quoted by Corita Kent in *Damn Everything but the Circus* (1970).

world is the birth of personality. And freedom gives rise to suffering. Refusal of personality, acquiescence in dissolution in the surrounding world can lessen the suffering, and man easily goes that way. . . ."[12]

Perhaps the most dramatic discovery of this fact was that of the prophet who out of the experience of exile and helplessness came to the conclusion that God suffers (Isa. 53:1–9). Experience of pleasure and happiness can no longer be identified with the divine. In a time when we are becoming so obsessed with immediate experience of pleasure, with apology for wonder, with the celebration of life, and with the joys of play, the symbol of the suffering Slave stands as a word of judgment. Our blindness to the tragic sense of life, our very incapacity to see tragedy when it is taking place, coupled with our anxiety to avoid suffering by plunging ourselves into the oblivion of satisfactions obtained by every kind of special stimulus, are signs of the decay of personality in our civilization, and of our growing despair as to the possibility of the creative act itself.

If suffering is the last word that personality has to say about life, then human life is nothing more than a fantastic mistake. But what is the magician saying, what is the child singing and the utopian visionary longing for? They all confess that happiness is the deepest of their desires and that they wait for a world in which it will triumph over the absurd reality. But if suffering is the last word of personality about life, then we have to agree with Freud. "The intention that man should be 'happy' is not included in the plan of 'Creation.' " [13] Therefore the only reasonable attitude in man is "the acknowledgement of his smallness and his submission to death as to all natural necessities in a spirit of resignation."[14] If this is the case, we have simply to

12. Nikolai Berdyaev, *Slavery and Freedom* (1944), p. 28.
13. Sigmund Freud, *Civilization and Its Discontents* (1962), p. 23.
14. Sigmund Freud, *Totem and Taboo* (1946), p. 115.

accept the absurdity of our desires and the finality of suffering, and to conclude that when evolution created man it committed a blunder. This, then, would be our civilization's final word on the matter.

There is another possibility, however, that is worth exploring. Why do I suffer? I suffer when I feel that our social order is structured in such a way that it has to destroy the values which are the ultimate concern of my personality. I suffer if I love freedom, but in order to survive have to prostitute my body to a system which yields only unfreedom. I suffer if I love peace and see that my nation, which has the power of life and death over me, creates and supports violence. I suffer if I love the free, innocent joy and beauty of nature, and see that the economy for which I work and on which I depend is destroying it.

Suppose that these contradictions between the values of personality and those that are built into our social system did not exist. I would be happy. Suffering arises when we discover that there is an insurmountable opposition between our own values and those of the world we live in. It is born in the moment when we come to the conclusion that we are homeless. It is the experience of meaninglessness, of our world's irreducible absurdity, of the futility of all efforts to make sense of it.

There is a radical difference between this kind of suffering and bodily pain. "A woman in labour is in pain because her time has come; but when the child is born she forgets the anguish in her joy that a man has been born into the world." There is a suffering that makes sense because it is necessary for the creation of our values. Grief is turned to joy (John 16:20–21). This is why it makes sense to be persecuted for the sake of what we hold to be noble and just. Man is ready to go to prison and to risk his life. He knows that these are the pains of childbirth. One may even die, but not in vain; for death itself makes sense. Think of the woman who knows she is barren—knows she will never go through the pangs of childbirth. Does that make her happy? Only if she hates children. She suffers, not because of pain, but because she will never experience the pain which announces that a new life is being born.

What makes personality suffer? Is it because it is inwardly deranged? Or because it contains a bundle of contradictory tendencies? Hardly. The essential and irreducible suffering of personality results from the fact that it is much more realistic than the realists. It knows the world in a way it is seldom consciously known. It knows that reality makes no room for its values—that the reasons of the heart have been displaced by the facts of power—and that the rationalization of power makes the creative act impossible. It knows the world from the vantage point of the future it envisages, and it hears the verdict clearly: those values must be aborted. To be happy in an unfriendly world is to be insane. The price of contentment, in such a situation, is to exchange reality for illusion.

Do you remember the story of the ugly duckling and how he found happiness by becoming a swan? Well, the story might have had a different ending. He might have found it by adapting himself.

These are the two alternatives for man. One may find joy by recreating the world in one's own image and likeness. Or one may produce a similar emotional condition by giving up one's dreams. If you accept the values which are built into the dominant institutional arrangements of our social order you will find yourself comfortably at home. The barren woman may refuse to give up her dream of having a baby and thus go on, through initial frustration and suffering, to solve her problem medically. Or she may come to the conclusion that to be happy now is more important than to be pregnant tomorrow. And thus she gives up her dream and looks for satisfaction elsewhere. In the first case joy exists because of and after a creative act. In the second, happiness is achieved by giving up the will to be creative. In the one case, she may celebrate, and dance and smile and experience the wonder that such a miracle is possible. In the other, happiness is the proof that she has become tame, barren, and domesticated.

We may now understand the reason why personality clings to its suffering. It suffers because it refuses false solutions—i.e., those that do not involve any change in reality but only a change in consciousness. These are "substitute-gratifications": since the world cannot be what personality desires, one gives up personality itself and puts on a "role," a new identity borrowed from the social system.

And why must personality suffer? It loves life too much. Life is its ultimate concern, for life itself created it. The suffering is a symptom that reality and life are not yet reconciled. And how does personality, the essential human being, mean to solve the problem? By recreating the world out of its love. This is the utopian dream behind everything it does. At present, however, it is no more than a dream and a vision. It is one of the "things that are not" (1 Cor. 1:28, RSV). Thus personality has a strange way of defining the world in which it lives. What is now labeled "reality" must pass away (Rev. 21:4). The fact that the present order creates suffering and reduces the reasons of the heart to helplessness nullifies its pretensions of being called a true reality. For personality, what is cannot be true. True Reality is now no more than a possibility which may and should come into being by a creative act. Suffering is the symptom that personality has not yet arrived, has not yet found its home. It passes through the present as through a pseudo reality which must be abolished if joy is to enter into the world. But if suffering disappears, the search comes to a halt—man no longer feels the need of a creative act, and the Reality which was being engendered is aborted.

The secret of realism is that it says happiness can be achieved without changing the world. It assumes that reality has already arrived, and that there is no basic contradiction between the heart and the present order of things. "Do you suffer? It is because you are still seeking. Give up your dreams. Adapt yourself to the pattern of the present world. All restlessness will disappear, and you will find yourself at home. There is no easier way of solving the feeling of discomfort and pain than by adapting oneself. Even mice are able to learn this simple lesson—why not man? Why knock our heads against reality in a hopeless attempt to transform it, if the emotional result attendant on the creative act can be achieved by a so much simpler and painless change in consciousness? Become adjusted and you will find happiness."

Freud described the neurotic as a person who gives too much attention to his emotions—he clings to his dreams as poor "substitute-gratifications" for what is already immediately available before him. The neurotic, Freud pointed out, values his emotions more than reality. But is not this what the realist does? He is so anxious to get rid of any discomfort, so anxious to find the nice feeling of happiness, that he accepts domestication, abandoning the insight that only through a creative act can true Reality come into being—abandoning this for the immediate gratification he can get from adapting to the given.

Since the birth of true Reality involves too much pain, he settles for the cheaper pleasure of being tame. Is not this a "substitute-gratification"? No longer a seeker, he is now one who has found. Happiness is achieved by effacing from consciousness the awareness of the problem. This is the magic of adjustment. It manages to dissolve the contradictions that exist in reality by means of a gimmick inside one's skull.

And this is why personality keeps its wounds open. They are a sign that one is alive, that one is still aware of something wrong in the order of things. Paraphrasing Wittgenstein, we may say that personality is a fight against the spell that so-called reality wants to put upon us. It denounces adjustment as a new form of the opiate of the people, and realism as a new illusion which dresses itself up in the garments of reality.

9

The Abortion of the Creative Possibility: Illusions

Imagination and personality cannot be separated, because personality is imagination made flesh. Whatever is true of personality must hold true for imagination also.

Imagination knows, although in an unconscious way, that the order of things we call reality is built upon irrational assumptions. Realism is blind to this fact. By setting itself up as the criterion of sanity, realism makes it impossible for man to see the absurdity which lies at the very foundations of our society.

What, then, would imagination call true Reality? From its point of view, Reality has not yet been born. Right now it is no more than a possibility and a hope. I have said that imagination is like a woman in travail, awaiting the birth of a new order of things. But this new order will not come about as a natural result of the unfolding present. The "present evil world" must come to an end, and then Reality will be born by the power of man's creative act. It will be a "new creation." Realism, which proclaims that the future is a development of what presently exists, is a form of illusion. It is the modern opiate of the people.

This is a rather odd statement. It goes against everything we used to believe in. It is revealing that in our common language we tend to use the words *imagination* and *illusion* interchangeably, as if they were synonymous. We do not know where imagination stops and illusions begin. We assume that there is no qualitative difference between them, and that they are no more than different names for two different forms of the same illness, i.e., our fear of reality.

This, at least, is how Freud understood their relationship. Why is it that man creates illusions? He answered this question by pointing to what seemed to him the irreducibly contradictory character of human existence. From the outset, man is split between his drives for pleasure and the impossibility of having them fulfilled in reality. "What decides the purpose of life," he says, "is simply the programme of the pleasure principle." But the fact is that "there is no possibility at all of its being carried through; all the regulations of the universe run counter to it." Confronted with the verdict of reality on the futility of his dreams, man commits an act of ultimate folly. He escapes from reality into the world that his desires have created in his mind.

This, according to Freud, explains how illusions are born. Just as the spider spins its web out of itself, man builds a world out of his wishes. Illusions are reifications of our drives for pleasure. Desires become things. Man transforms wishes into reality, while reality itself is wished away into nothingness. For all practical purposes, man's illusions become the only world that counts. Encapsulated inside himself, he finds the reassuring feeling of being omnipotent and safe, of being master over the situation and having the world under control. Illusions give him what the world has denied. This is why they are substitute-gratifications. But Freud moves a step further and places the whole sphere of values, and therefore of imagination, under the same ban as illusions. "One thing only do I know for certain," he remarked, "and that is that man's judgements of value follow directly from his wishes for happiness—that accordingly they are an attempt to support his illusions with arguments."[1] Prophets and false prophets are thus nothing more than different forms of the same madness.

I want to suggest that this is not the case. If we are to understand the problem, we must start by realizing that *the relation between imagination and illusions is as conflicting and opposite as that between the true and the false prophet, because while imagination is committed to true Reality, illusions want to preserve a false one.*

Illusions are not produced by a crazy mind just for "kicks." As we all know, human life does not exist in a vacuum. We survive to the extent that we are able to interact with our natural environment, through the mediation of the society to which we belong. It is this complex network of relationships that gives birth to consciousness, which emerges from society and reflects its actual conditions. No matter what form it takes, our conscious life is always a symptom of the existential situation in which the struggle for survival takes place. Thus illusions, even when they seem totally disconnected from reality, have their roots in society. They are symptoms of concrete problems that life faces in its desperate effort to continue. If we want to understand illusions we must ask about the social conditions which have made their appearance possible and necessary. As Marx once pointed out, the existence of illusions is a sign that underneath them are social conditions which *need* illusions. The illusions themselves are an indication that the social order is sick. This suggests that the riddle of the individual's mental derangement is ultimately to be solved in terms of the social pathology which has left him without alter-

1. Sigmund Freud, *Civilization and Its Discontents* (1962), pp. 23, 92.

natives. We need first to diagnose the illness of our times.

The past two decades have been the years when we were expelled from paradise. Our innocence was lost. We had been brought up carefully protected by the illusions past generations had created. They gave meaning to our world, and we felt that life made sense because wherever we looked we saw that institutions were the embodiment of our aspirations. One did not feel any need to protest, even less to rebel. We did not know what it meant to be exiles, for we experienced our world as a friendly home.

But then, suddenly, we began to discover that there was something irrational at the very foundations of our civilization. The destitute nations of the world were the first to perceive this, perhaps because suffering, oppression, and exploitation have the effect of forcing man to see deeper and think with greater passion, in circumstances where seeing and thinking become matters of survival. America had never had this experience. Hollywood created such deep habitual ruts of thought in the American mind that one came to assume as a matter of course that every tragedy had a happy ending. This is why as late as in the early sixties the dominant mood in this country was still that of the "silent generation" of the fifties. So powerful were the dominant illusions that they crumbled only under the impact of the tragedy of Vietnam. And then, one after another, they fell from their pedestals.

That was a moment of truth. A painful one. We saw with horror that our affluence and comfort were built upon violence, genocide, earlier slavery, and exploitation and greed. And with this discovery came the vision that the world must and could be transformed, and that this was the task of our generation to carry through. A period of feverish political activity followed. Revolutionaries and prophets were born, filled with the confidence that their power was enough to break the old values and create new ones.

But their hopes were never fulfilled. The certainty that they were the vanguard of an apocalyptic time which would bring to an end the present evil world was followed by the sudden discovery that they were trapped, powerless, and captive. Their heroes were killed. And the sweet taste of their vanishing hopes mixed with the bitterness of unexpected frustrations. The meaning of their political experience was unequivocal: *the creative act was impossible.* Why? *Because they were powerless.*

But one cannot go through this experience and remain whole. How could they forget their utopian dreams? The tension is unbearable. Personality is split between aspiration and frustration, between hopes and the hard reality of power. The suffering must be obliterated. And how is this to be accomplished? Consciousness performs a magical trick. It takes hold of its experience that *action is no longer possible* and translates it to mean: *action is no longer necessary.* The problem of reality is dissolved in illusion.

Thus illusions are born when one discovers that the creative act involves pain, suffering, endurance, and postponement of pleasure. Very often life itself is included in the risk. But this runs counter to our comfortable habits!

For the sake of present satisfactions man decides to forget his love. Why go through the pains of pregnancy and the pangs of childbirth? It is easier simply to get fatter. Consciousness thus resolves the ethical urgency of a creative act by means of a gimmick: it proclaims to itself, with great seriousness, that the act is unnecessary. This is what false prophecy is all about. False prophets are professionals of illusion.

> Prophets and priests are frauds,
>   every one of them;

> they dress my people's wound, but skin-deep only,
>   with their saying: 'All is well.'
> All well? Nothing is well! [Jer. 8:10-11]

See how the miracle is performed? The wound is still there. Everything remains the same. But by a linguistic trick the contradiction is dissolved, and "all is well." But the problem is that what consciousness tells itself does not correspond to reality. "Nothing is well." Therefore,

> Do not listen to what the prophets say,
> who buoy you with false hopes;
> the vision they report springs from their own imagination,
>   it is not from the mouth of the Lord. [Jer. 23:16]

Men are made happy. By the power of positive thinking everything is possible. The thorn is pulled out of the flesh. They no longer feel the discomfort they should feel, if they were truly aware of the reality in which they live. Suffering disappears. One no longer needs to feel an exile. How are they saved from pain? By becoming insensitive. Illusions are thus built upon a strange arithmetic: they add by subtracting. What they give, in terms of wish-fulfillment, comes from what they take away in terms of awareness. The greater the awareness, the greater the pain. It follows logically that the less the awareness, the greater the pleasure. As popular wisdom puts it, "The heart cannot feel what the eye cannot see."

This is why *The Greening of America* has had such a tremendous appeal. It announces birth without pregnancy, a new world without the pains and risks of a political struggle.

There is a revolution coming. It will not be like the revolutions of the past. It will originate with the individual and with culture, and it will change the political structure only as its final act. It promises a higher reason, a more human community, and a new and liberated individual. Its ultimate creation will be a new and enduring wholeness and beauty

—a renewed relationship of man to himself, to other men, to society, to nature, and to the land. Today we are witnesses to a great moment in history: a turn from the pessimism that has closed in on modern industrial society; the rebirth of a future; the rebirth of a people in a sterile land. If that process had to be summed up in a single word, that word would be freedom.[2]

This is the language of an oracle who has seen the future. No doubts—only certainties. Who would not like to believe his vision?

A new message is then proclaimed: resurrection is possible without the cross. "The next generation needs to be told that the real fight is not a political fight," announces Norman O. Brown. The task is "to put an end to politics." "From politics to poetry. . . . Poetry, art, imagination, the creator spirit is life itself; the real revolutionary power to change the world."[3] He does not speak in his own name. Indeed, the power of Brown's preaching has to do with the fact that he puts into words what a frustrated generation is feeling. Helplessness gives birth to despair of power, and with it the hope of a magic panacea: to create by thought what one could not create with one's hands. If Roszak is correct in describing the counter-culture as "an exploration of the politics of consciousness,"[4] then it is bewitched by this illusion. "Consciousness is capable of changing and of destroying the Corporate State, without violence, without seizure of political power, without the overthrow of any existing group of people. The new generation, by experimenting with action on the level of consciousness, has shown the way to the one method of change that will work in today's postindustrial society: changing consciousness."[5]

2. Charles A. Reich, *The Greening of America* (1971), pp. 2, 379.
3. Quoted by Theodore Roszak in *The Making of a Counter Culture* (1969), p. 118.
4. *Ibid.*, p. 156.
5. Reich, *op. cit.*, pp. 322, 327.

I agree that traditional politics must be abolished. It has functioned as a means whereby people avoided the suffering involved in being responsible for the world, but delegating their power to a group of professionals. One is then free for fishing, bridge, and golf. Traditional politics must be abolished because it justifies the monopoly of power of the few over the many, thereby rendering the many incapable of being directly involved in the creative act. The direct creative act has been relegated to the sphere of illegality. Moreover, traditional politics makes a truly creative act impossible. We have seen that creativity requires giving up long-held presuppositions in order to start anew—death and resurrection. In traditional politics, no matter which party wins, the rules remain the same. If you play chess with an opponent, your accidental opposition presupposes a basic agreement as to the rules of the game. This is why Jesus refused to play the political game. "Is it permissible to pay tax to Caesar?" (In language we would understand today, "Whose side are you on?") Jesus refused to play the game. He had no desire to see his face stamped on the chips of a game now controlled by Caesar. If he had, business would have gone on as usual. His purpose was not to win that game but to abolish it.

True, the counter-culture has perceived something that both liberals and revolutionaries have overlooked. It has gone deeper into the sources of our sickness. But can one move from this point to the conclusion that the world can be changed without power? The Slaves have seen that if they play the game of the Masters they will always remain Slaves. Ought they then to conclude that power is useless and self-defeating?

Don't misunderstand me. I do not believe that a new world can be created without utopian dreams. The magician, the child, the prophet, the visionary, the artist— they all live by the revolution which has already taken place in their consciousnesses. But their visions must function in life as an *aperitif*—as the announcement of what is to come. They must be like the preliminaries of love: the body is roused for the great act which can be the beginning of a pregnancy. If caressing becomes an end in itself, it is nothing more than masturbation: it gives shallow pleasure without fertilizing. And this is the danger of the politics of consciousness, which proclaims that one can enjoy now, in all its fullness, something that does not yet exist. It announces redemption of an unredeemed world, celebration when life is still groaning in travail, play in a world built upon war.

Perhaps we should recall the parable Marx once told of those who, in his day, proclaimed the same message of politics of consciousness.

Once upon a time an honest fellow had the idea that men were drowned in water only because they were possessed with the idea of gravity. If they were to knock this idea out of their heads, say by stating it to be a superstition, a religious idea, they would be sublimely proof against any danger from water. His whole life long he fought against the illusion of gravity, of whose harmful results all statistics brought him new and manifold evidence. This honest fellow was the type of the new revolutionary philosophers in Germany.[6]

One might add: and of the new illusionists of revolution through consciousness.

The politics of consciousness is an illusion. In what way is it basically different from the power of positive thinking? The pietists, too, once promised: "Transform the individual and society will be changed." It is rather intriguing that this pattern recurs over and over again in American (and why not say Western?) history. Idealism draws us with an irresistible attraction. It dominates churches and the world of scholarship, individuals and communities.

6. Karl Marx and Friedrich Engels, *The German Ideology* (1947), p. 2.

The reason? I do not know. But I have an inkling. Americans have learned that results must be achieved quickly. Pregnancies must be quick. One plants pumpkins because in six months they will become pies. Plant dates? What a crazy idea! As the saying goes, "He who plants dates will not eat them." Americans cannot stand the frustration that goes with failure. For them this is an unbearable psychological strain. Their hope does not go beyond reach of their eyes; this is why they are soft and lack endurance (cf. Rom. 8:25). To suffer now with one's heart set on the land of one's grandchildren, as Nietzsche proposes, is not a viable psychological alternative for them. Shortcuts must be found. And this is the miracle that consciousness performs: it puts the yet unborn child into the arms of would-be parents. They play, dance, and rejoice. Pregnancy is no longer needed. They do not realize that it is not a real baby, but a doll (maybe a Barbie doll).

If the future is sure, one is absolved from the suffering and discipline required by the creative act. No longer the moment of planting the seeds of one's highest hopes and then watering them with tears, sweat, and blood. The present becomes a time of playing and dancing, of enjoyment and celebration, of wonder and awe.

Beneath all this gaiety lurks the ghost of despair. Man has despaired of himself as creator. The way out: to redefine himself as one primarily concerned with immediate experience. If I cannot create with the body, let me feel with the body! It is interesting to notice that Nietzsche, prophet of the body and the Dionysian style of life, was aware of the fact that there is no joy for the body if it cannot create a new meaning for the earth. I suspect that there is no basic difference between "Let us eat and drink and play, for the Messiah will come," and "Let us eat, drink and be merry, for tomorrow we die." Nihilism and the abolition of politics are branches of the same tree. They are the sigh of an oppressed creature, the cry of the helpless, the celebration of joy by those who have despaired of creating it.

For there is another way of finding happiness. If your dreams make you suffer, forget them. Be tame. There is beginning to be talk about "the cooling of America." What is this if not a process of becoming "mature"—of defining one's hopes as utopian and becoming realistic and normal again? Once we were like wild ducks, beating our wings, flying high up in the skies, facing danger and fatigue—permanent emigrants, always moving from one place to another. But then we looked down and saw a flock of happy, fat domestic ducks, and we envied them. We joined them and became as they are.

Alas, the time has come when man will no longer give birth to a star. Alas, the time of the most despicable man has come, he that is no longer able to despise himself. Behold, I show you the *last* man. . . .

"What is love? What is creation? What is longing? What is a star?" Thus asks the last man, and he blinks.

"We have invented happiness," say the last men, and they blink. . . . No shepherd and one herd! Everybody wants the same, everybody is the same: whoever feels differently goes voluntarily into a madhouse.[7]

Indeed, we have joined the Masters. We are protected under their strong eagle wings. "Relax, domestic duck. Enjoy your fatness. But do not try to spread your wings again . . ."

Slaves build illusions as a way of effacing the pain of their impotence. The Blacks created spirituals; the oppressed indulge in dreams of a future paradise; the weak give birth to a strong God. Illusions are ways of blotting out the suffering that comes from the awareness that *they cannot change the world*.

With the Masters it is just the other way round. They have the monopoly of power. They control the geography of pain and pleasure. The world is good for them. Therefore they want to preserve it. Their illusions express the fact that *they do not want to change the world.* They must therefore avoid seeing the suffering on which their pleasure is built. They twist their noses so as not to smell the odor of decay that comes out of the world's wounds. They close their eyes and ears so as not to see or hear the screams of pain, revolt, and hatred of those whom they oppress, taking great care not to know anything about oppression. And they keep saying one to another: "How rich I am! And how well I have done! I have everything I want"—unable to see that they are "the most pitiful wretches, poor, blind, and naked" (Rev. 3:17). They want to preserve. The present satisfies them and becomes the model of the future. They must be realistic. But they cannot see that their realism is nothing more than a way of affirming their own condition of Master.

This is why Toffler's *Future Shock* is so appealing. He is the priest who announces that there is nothing wrong, that tomorrow will be better than today, and by preserving the fundamental power structures of our civilization we shall reach an undreamed-of future. The secret of modularism is that the Master must remain.

Reich articulates the illusions of the oppressed, and Toffler the illusions of the oppressors. The former proclaims that the creative political act is no longer necessary. The latter announces that the creative political act is no longer possible. And by this means they join together Slaves and Masters into a single system. If the Slave agrees that the creative act is no longer needed, he is unconsciously acknowledging the Master's claim that it is no longer possible. Their former opposition is resolved into a single mode of operating. Things remain as they are.

Strange as it may be, the fact is that many symbolic universes which appear totally opposed to the status quo actually function for its preservation. Many years ago Karl Mannheim remarked that "representatives of a given order have not in all cases taken a hostile attitude towards orientations transcending the existing order," as is the case with the illusions of the Slave. "Rather they have always aimed to control these situationally transcendent ideas and interests which are not realizable within the bounds of the present order, and thereby to render them socially impotent."[8] Illusions must be understood from *the way they function* and not from what they say. Instead of abolishing the real contradictions of social life through a creative act, they dissolve the ethical demand for it. By proclaiming the inevitability (or impossibility—either one) of the happy ending, they make it possible for business to go on as usual. And my impression is that this is how the politics of consciousness functions: if the creative act is no longer necessary, the truth of the values toward which it is aimed is reduced to impotence and made innocuous.

The actual condition of the Slave is that of being literally possessed by the demonic power of the Master. Impotent in the grip of pain, the Slave has the illusion of being an object of demonic possession. Reality is his enemy, cruel and powerful. What chances have *his* desires of becoming reality? None. But he cannot live without desires. His dreams of freedom, of happiness, of love—what does he do with them? He builds idols, i.e., he begins to behave *as if* they were already real—in a sphere beyond: beyond the river, beyond death, beyond the horizon. The idolatry of the Slave is the opiate he creates to liberate him from the actual demonic possession that controls his life.

With the Master the situation is just the reverse. His basic experience is not that of impotent pain but of omnipotent pleasure. His ultimate concern, therefore, becomes the preservation of things as they are. And he creates idols. These, for him,

8. Karl Mannheim, *Ideology and Utopia* (1936), p. 173.

are the expression of his actual conditions of life. He sees himself as the embodiment of goodness, justice, and truth. And the groans of pain and protest that reach his ears are like the sounds of a diabolical orgy. His love for his idols leads him to see in anyone who opposes him a demon who wants to destroy his cosmos.

Idolatry and demonic possession never exist in isolation. They are complementary expressions of the absurdity of the human condition which is perpetuated by the present order of things.

Illusions are not derangements of the mind. They are symptoms of concrete social conditions. They are indications that man is living in a world where creativity has been made impossible. They are symbolic representations of a disease and frustrated attempts to solve it. Although their prescription must be rejected, the social sickness that produces them must none the less be healed. If illusions were extemporaneous products of consciousness, they could be defeated by consciousness itself. But since they are products of a social situation, it is only through the removal of that situation that man can recover his sanity. As Marx put it, "The demand to give up illusions is the demand to give up the condition which needs illusions. It is necessary to pluck out the imaginary flowers from the chain not so that man will wear the chain without any fantasy or consolation but so that he will shake off the chain and cull the living flower."[9] Man must be disillusioned. To what end? In order to become realist? No. In order to abolish the reality that made his illusions necessary.

In the prophetic tradition demons are not enlightened. They are expelled. Idols are not converted; they are destroyed. The origin of the insanity of illusions is the insanity of power. The hope of a new future for man, therefore, depends on the possi-

9. Karl Marx and Friedrich Engels, *On Religion* (1964), p. 42.

bility of destroying idols and expelling demons. The dominant conditions of power must be abolished, for hope comes from creativity, and creativity requires a free space and free time in which man can shape the world according to the dreams of his heart. In short: psychoanalysis must go beyond itself. It must become politics.

10

The Child of Imagination: Culture and the Humanization of the World

We live in the entrails of a monster.

Smoke, speed, noise, blinking lights, the tyranny of clocks, the pressures of production and consumption, the need of accomplishment, atomic tests—this is our world. As a friend of mine once said, "They have mixed fear with the air," so that no matter how far you go you feel that our space and our time are polluted with hatred, violence, and greed."

Is this really our home? Hardly. We already begin to experience the sense of boredom and helplessness that animals develop in their cages. We move behind bars, going places in order to be reassured that the doors are still open. But it is useless. We are men without alternatives. We are possessed by powers that we hate, but against which there is nothing that we can do.

Perhaps this is why we are beginning to feel an obsessive nostalgia for nature. How we would like to be like a child in a meadow, with blue skies overhead, feeling the caressing breeze on our faces and hearing the murmur of brooks and the rustling of the trees. Nature gives us the feeling of openness, of spaces still unexplored, of horizons filled with alternatives. Nature has become a symbol for our lost freedom and a dream of our vanishing life. This is why we regard it with a mixture of mystical awe and of aesthetic ecstasy.

Our desires, however, tend to romanticize it—and again we create an illusion. We forget that the sunset is beautiful only if we are not hungry, do not feel pain, are not lost on a desert, and have a cozy place to go when darkness falls. Beautiful sunsets and breathtaking landscapes are strangely insensitive to pain and tragedy. Nature lacks a heart. It is unable to love. With the same meticulous insensitivity as it creates the most delicate flower, it mercilessly crushes the weak. Nature freely helps no form of life. It serves only those who have power to force it to serve them.

There is the child on the meadow! Nothing more simple, natural, and beautiful. Behind that scene, however, is a long, almost forgotten story: life struggling against nature in order to survive. The unfit and weak disappearing. Only forms of life that prove fit manage to stay alive. This holds true all the way from the amoeba to man.

But we are speaking of an abstraction. Have you ever seen life? No. What we see are living organisms: plants, insects, frogs, men. Organisms result from a long process of experimentation. Some experiments fail, and those forms of life disappear. Others succeed in inventing and learning adequate solutions for the problem of life's relation to nature. They survive.

Every species accumulates a body of knowledge through its successes and failures. They are able to create recipes for survival in a physical universe which shows no kindness to life. Each organism thus preserves a unique history and contains a set of solutions which have emerged out of its life experience. To an amoeba, a flea, a mouse, a cat, a buzzard, a shrimp, an octopus, the problem of survival is not the same. For each the riddle of life is different, and the solutions to it are as varied as the organisms. An animal's body can be understood as a long learning process which eventually became a biological structure. It is the memory of solutions invented in the past. Its body tells an animal what it has to do in order to find a friendly environment in an unfriendly nature. The environment is the part of nature that functions, for the animal, according to its bodily needs. Anatomical structure is like the model of a gigantic jigsaw puzzle—a replica of the world around it—and its world must be an extension of it. "An organism can exist only if it succeeds in finding in the world an adequate environment —in shaping an environment." But this environment is not given by nature. It does not make room for life. "The environment emerges from the world through the being or actualization of the organism."[1]

The variety of recipes for survival exhibit a common logic of life—they have a common denominator. All animals manage to survive by adapting their bodies to nature. It is as if life on this level had come to the conclusion that nature is an insurmountable obstacle which cannot be transformed. Here life is more realistic than anywhere else. It accepts the rules of the game, and by becoming expert at it manages to find itself a space where it can survive. Animals survive by *naturalizing* themselves. This is the basic wisdom that every new generation of animals reenacts throughout its life.

This is why animals have been doing identical things for thousands and thousands of years, without ever coming to any creative change or seeming bored by what they do. Animals *are* and *do* what the past of their species programs them to be and do. They cannot invent new ways of being. The possibilities of their

1. Kurt Goldenstein, *The Organism* (1963), p. 88.

future are limited by past experience. A creative act implies the abandonment of past assumptions, but since for animals these assumptions are built into their own bodies, creativity would imply death. They are thus condemned to be prisoners of their past and to go on repeating the ways of being and acting which have emerged out of their past history. Animals cannot be different tomorrow from what they were yesterday.

The human world also begins with the body. "In the beginning was the Body . . ." Everything man has created—his tools, society, values, aspirations, hopes, memories, myths, language, religion, ideologies, science, and whatever else we might catalogue as having come from man—has been engendered in the midst of his struggle for survival. All his inventions have been created by the body, for the sake of the body. To represent the human world in a graphic form one might draw a large circle containing everything man has produced. And right in the middle, as the source and reason of it all—as the hot spot of the human world, its structuring center and emotional matrix: man's body. The body is the origin of the categorical imperative of acting in order to live. Or more precisely: acting in order to live with satisfaction. The body has thus an axiological priority over everything else, because it is the foundation and goal of the human world.

This is not what we used to be told. Our civilization is based on the assumption that true humanity begins where the body comes to an end. Erasmus expressed in a terse way the spirit of our world when he denounced the body as a whore.[2] We learned that mind, intellect, spirit, and soul are the essence of man. The body is their prison. It is like a stone tied to the eagle, so that it cannot fly.

Wherever we go, the spirit of repression of the body is pre-

2. Few people realize that it was in opposition to this suicidal philosophy of life that Luther declared that reason, and not the body, is the real whore.

sent. It dominates the so-called "learned community." Orozco has shown it in a mural depicting a college commencement. There is the scholar! He is the symbol of the highest achievements of mind in our society. His body has shrunk. His human likeness is lost. That is what the discipline of scholarship creates: hours and hours sitting down, hours and hours with all the bodily senses turned off and only the intellect in operation, hours and hours locked inside his study with its desk, shelves, books. The look of death is already on his face. Now, the moment of glory! He is going to grant the symbol of intellectual excellence to his disciple, who has mastered the intricacies of scholarship and has become just like his master. And he receives the diploma: a test tube with a dead fetus inside.

This is the spirit that dominates our churches. See how people close their eyes when they pray. They do not know why. It has become an automatic reflex. But the reason is that they believe God begins where the body ends. The act of closing one's eyes is an act of refusal of the body and of rejection of the world. Deep inside, in the inner sphere of the intellect: there is where God is to be found. Nietzsche was right when he remarked scornfully that "the saint in whom God delights is the ideal eunuch. Life has come to an end where the 'Kingdom of God' begins."[3]

But more than that, the fact is that rationalization and efficiency, the very foundations of our civilization, cannot exist without repression of the body. For man to become a function of the system, he must repress all the natural rhythms that belong to his body and begin to operate according to the rhythm which the system itself establishes. Play and efficiency do not go together. As you look at your watch, as you run to take the commuter train or subway, enter the factory or the aseptic

3. Friedrich Nietzsche, *Twilight of the Idols*, in Walter Kaufmann, ed., *The Portable Nietzsche* (1968), p. 490.

world of the bureaucrat, everything repeats the same refrain: "The body must be overcome."

But whatever goes against the body goes against the most fundamental presuppositions of life—hence this process cannot go on indefinitely. Whenever it is repressed, the body begins to groan and protest against all ideas, principles, values, systems, institutions, and organizations that use it as if it were a means. But the body is never a means, it is always an end. This is why perhaps the deepest of all its aspirations is that of freedom from repression. As Paul put it, "We . . . are groaning inwardly while we wait for God to . . . set our whole body free" (Rom. 8:23). Or as Orwell once put it, "On the battlefield, in the torture chamber, on a sinking ship, the issues that you are fighting for are always forgotten, because the body swells up until it fills the universe, and even when you are not paralyzed by fright or screaming with pain, life is a moment-to-moment struggle against hunger or cold or sleeplessness, against a sour stomach or an aching tooth."[4]

Our civilization has tried to convince us that this is not so, that the greater the repression of the body, the greater the freedom of the spirit. It is ironical that torturers have known more about man than our ideologues. For millenia they have known that whoever controls the body has power also over personality. Personality is a function of the body, and whenever it is unable either to resolve or provide a meaning for suffering, it falls apart. Berdyaev perceived this fact very clearly. "The rights of the human body," he remarked, "are bound up with the value of personality." "The most shocking encroachments upon personality are in the first place encroachments upon the body. It is first of all the human body that they starve, beat and kill, and through the body this process spreads to the whole man."[5]

4. George Orwell, *Nineteen Eighty Four* (1949), p. 102.
5. Nikolai Berdyaev, *Slavery and Freedom* (1944), p. 32.

A civilization which is built upon the repression of the body and its transformation into a means for its own ends—a process which ranges from the subtle scientific conditioning of behavior to the most brutal forms of torture and violence—is the very embodiment of death and madness, and is doomed to end up by abolishing life itself.

We must return to the body. There is no other way to recover the meaning of life and to discover what it means to be and to act as a human being.

I have mentioned that animals manage to survive by becoming experts in the operations they are programed to perform. Their bodies became tools, with amazing abilities to run, jump, dig, fly, kill, disguise themselves. Nothing like that has happened to man. Our bodies are remarkable for their clumsiness. Our greatest Olympic feats are laughable when compared with what ants, kangaroos, grasshoppers, and antelopes normally do.

Our body did not become a tool. Therefore we had to invent them. Tools are extensions of the body. And among them— possibly before any others—man created society. This also is a tool. Alone, man could not survive. To come together, work together, devise a division of labor: that was practical expediency for the sake of survival.

Society is not specifically human. Bees and ants have highly organized forms of social life, with precise divisions of labor and a very well-defined complex of tasks to be carried out. It would be possible to analyze human society from this angle alone. We could take its organization, stratification, programed tasks, ends which are built into the social system—and we would have before us the picture of a structure understood from the angle of what it does in order to survive. This has been the most persistent tendency of our social sciences, which Mannheim has described as the displacement of politics by economy. Society is understood as an *order of efficacy*, totally controlled by the pragmatic motive.

But this is not the whole truth about the human world. Man is not an improved ant or a larger bee. If we took seriously the claims of realism, ants and bees should be placed ahead of man in the scale of life, for they are perfect realists and pragmatic through and through. There is no deviant behavior among them. No revolutionaries, no visionaries, no rebels, no neurotics. They follow relentlessly the program which is built into their biological structure. They are totally adjusted "normal" beings. Their "consciousness" is a replica of their social organization.

But this is not true for man. If man were a creature whose behavior was tightly programed by the stimuli-response pattern, and therefore no more than one animal among others, he would find satisfaction in sheer physical survival. But this is not the case. There is nothing further from his intentions than a pragmatic attitude solely concerned with efficiency. It is very revealing that there are circumstances in which man—in spite of the fact that he enjoys good health and even affluence, a situation which appears totally adequate from a pragmatic point of view—decides to drop out, join a commune, become a revolutionary, be a hermit, or even commit suicide. Why? Because in the logic of personality it is not possible to equate economic well-being with happiness and human fulfillment. As was said long ago (and forgotten by the priests of economic development and modernization), man does not live by bread alone.

Then what is man after when, in spite of having everything, he decides to give it up and be poor, or to risk his life or even end it? He is after meaning. Man needs to live in a world that makes sense. As we have seen, this is what the magician, the child, and the utopian visionary are saying. Personality is not a function of economy. To survive, it must be able to see its values embodied in the world around it. As Werner Stark remarks, "Before other 'interests' can claim satisfaction, one basic 'interest' must be satisfied—namely, the necessity of living in an understandable universe."[6] What is an understandable universe? Is it the reality constructed by science? If this were so, scientists would be the absolute prototypes of humanity. But this is hardly the case. When do we say that something makes sense? It is when we feel that our structure of values is being confirmed by our experience. *Future Shock* does not make sense to me. It makes me suffer. Because I hate the values it proclaims. *The Little Prince* makes sense to me. It makes me happy. Because I find there someone who lives and loves the values that are dear to me. Personality needs more than physical ecology. It requires something one might call cultural ecology, i.e., a world which embodies and exhibits the aspirations of the heart.

One of the most moving expressions of what the world of culture means may be found in a conversation between the little prince and his friend, the fox.

"My life is very monotonous," said the fox. "I hunt chickens; men hunt men. All the chickens are just alike, and all men are just alike. And, in consequence, I am a little bored. But if you tame me, it will be as if the sun came to shine on my life. I shall know the sound of a step that will be different from all others. Other steps send me hurrying back underneath the ground. Yours will call me, like music, out of my burrow. And then look: you see the grain-fields down yonder? I do not eat bread. Wheat is of no use to me. And that is sad. But you have hair that is the color of gold. Think how wonderful that will be when you have tamed me! The grain, which is also golden, will bring me back the thought of you. And I shall love to listen to the wind in the wheat . . ."

6. Werner Stark, *The Sociology of Knowledge* (1967), p. 50.

So the little prince tamed the fox. And when the hour of his departure drew near—

"Ah," said the fox, "I shall cry."

"It is your own fault," said the little prince. "I never wished you any sort of harm; but you wanted me to tame you . . ."

"Yes," said the fox.

"But now you are going to cry!" said the little prince.

"Yes, that is so," said the fox.

"Then it has done you no good at all!"

"It has done me good," said the fox, "because of the color of the wheat fields."

And then the fox tells the little prince his secret, precisely the secret that our spiritless civilization cannot understand: "It is only with the heart that one can see rightly; what is essential is invisible to the eye."[7]

Chicken and hunters, the world of practical problems where the issue of biological survival is decided, do not suffice. The fox is unhappy. Something is still missing. But suddenly a magic transformation takes place. More chickens and less hunters? No. The fox is tamed. His world finds a new center. And things that were totally meaningless before—the wheat and the wind—become sacraments. They become symbols of something that cannot be seen but makes all the difference between boredom and humanity. The world gains a personal center. It becomes charged with meaning, filled with possibilities of suffering and joy.

Is that too poetic? Does it sound too romantic?

Let us turn to Henri Lefebvre. He is a scientist. To be more precise, a Marxist scientist. He tells us, in the respectable language of science, what the fox says in the language of poetry. "Human action does not endeavor to produce objects only. It wants to create a *higher order*. Its intention is to produce unlim-

7. Antoine de Saint-Exupéry, *The Little Prince* (1943), pp. 83, 86–87.

ited pleasure. [Ah! The dream of the magician! The message of play!] It wants to create voluptuousness without pain and mistake. The human being, as he tries to dominate the external world is really attempting to take possession of his internal nature."[8] Tools must be more than tools; technology more than technology; economy more than economy; power more than power! They must be instruments of human intention, the hands of the heart.

This theme recurs over and over again in the young Marx. It is a pity that most of what we know of him are the caricatures of those who did not understand him. He was vulgarized as a crude materialist who reduced life to economics. Few have noticed that for him economics has very little to do with money. When he says that the basis of life is the economy he is pointing to the fact that the human world begins with the transformation of nature. "Men must be in a position to live in order to make history," he says. "But life involves before everything else eating and drinking, a habitation, clothing and many other things. The first historical act is thus the production of the means to satisfy these needs, the production of material life itself."[9]

The ape becomes man when he begins to transform nature. But is this not also true of animals? They build nests, dams, webs. The qualitative difference that distinguishes what man does from what animals do is that man transcends biological determinism and creates out of freedom and imagination. "It is true that 'animals also produce.' They produce only under the compulsion of direct physical need, while man produces when he is free from physical need, and only truly produces in freedom from such need. Animals construct in accordance with the standards and needs of the species to which they belong, while

8. Henri Lefebvre, *Le Langage et la Société* (1966), pp. 310–11. My translation.
9. Karl Marx and Friedrich Engels, *The German Ideology* (1947), p. 16.

man knows how to produce in accordance with the laws of beauty."[10] Thus man is not seeking only the satisfaction of his biological needs. He looks for meaning. He longs for joy. He wants to shape the world into his image and likeness, in order to "see his own reflection in a world which he has constructed."[11] It is important to feed his body. But that does not suffice. The heart must be happy. What man creates must have more than its obvious practical function. Gross national product and economic growth are not enough. Bread must be more than bread. Production must bring joy and psychic satisfaction. It must be a sacrament.

It is clear why Marx was so critical of capitalist society. The problem was not that it was not efficient enough. He does not propose a different recipe for the same pudding. The problem was that it had become so materialistic that production could only be measured in terms of money. The creative act had no role to play. Indeed, the creative act had been made impossible. Instead of being the child of man's freedom and therefore the highest expression of life itself, work has become nothing more than a "means for the satisfaction of a need." "Life appears only as a means to life."[12] And the worker, consequently, cannot enjoy work as play. He finds no psychic fulfillment in it. Marx is saying that the "order of efficacy" of our society implies a regression into a kind of logic that life itself rejected when it gave birth to man. Animals are totally pragmatic. They produce in order to survive. Man, however, has stepped above this level. Besides survival, he needs to build a world that makes sense. This is why he created culture. Culture is the union of love and power, or more precisely, it is the power of love assuming a

10. Karl Marx, "Alienated Labor," in Erich Fromm, *Marx's Concept of Man* (1964), p. 102.
11. *Ibid.*, p. 102.
12. *Ibid.*, p. 101.

social form. It is a synthesis between effectiveness and imagination in which the heart succeeds in forcing the system to be an instrument for its realization and a means for its expression. Jaeger and Selznick summarize the whole process in a beautiful way. "The culture-creating act," they say, "is more than an emotional response, surely more than a flight, more also than a manipulative gambit. It is an effort to make the world rich with personal significance, to place the inner self upon the stage, to transform narrow instrumental roles into vehicles of psychic fulfillment. It implicates the self and strives to invest the environment with subjective relevance and meaning. In an older tradition," they conclude, "we might have referred to this investment as 'the objectification of the spirit.' "[13] The "Spirit" takes the formless chaos and gives it a shape derived from its aspirations, so that the result produces that experience of aesthetic fulfillment: "It is very good!" Genuine culture, remarked Sapir, is "inherently harmonious, balanced, self-satisfactory, in which nothing is spiritually meaningless."[14] It has the meaning of play, as Huizinga pointed out, and the significance of a work of art, as Dewey clearly perceived.

To recapitulate the comparison: animals survive by adapting to nature. *Man adapts nature to himself.* Animals are naturalized. *Man humanizes nature.* There it is, threatening, alien, heartless, resistant! Man takes nature in his hands, and the miracle occurs. It becomes *for* man. And then, but only then, he experiences his own naturalism. He is free to go back to nature, because through his creative act it has become his friend and his home.

Animals are prisoners of their bodies. Their power of production is determined by the past of their species, which now con-

13. Gertrud Jaeger and Phillip Selznick, "A Normative Theory of Culture" (1964), p. 685.
14. *Ibid.*, p. 666.

trols them through their biological structure. They have no alternatives. They have to do today and will do tomorrow what was decided by their past history. They cannot create; they repeat. Looking at a nest, we know what bird made it. Looking at a cobweb, we know what kind of spider constructed it. And inversely, just by looking at an animal we already know the plot of its whole life.

When we enter the sphere of culture, however, we discover that a totally different logic is at work. True, cultures are created out of bodily needs, and they are built by the power of the body. But it is not possible to find any causal relation between man's biological structure and the culture he builds. As Kroeber puts it, culture is behavior "that is independent of the genetic constitutions and biological characteristics of organism."[15]

How can we account for this variety of products coming from the same biological structure? The answer is simple. Man is not programed by his body. His past does not hold him captive. Animals, controlled by their past, are closed. With man this is not so. He is open. He is an unfinished experiment. Although conditioned by his past, he is not condemned to go on repeating and reenacting it in rigidly repetitive fashion. He has the unique possibility of *using* his past as a tool for the creation of a qualitatively new future. Man's physical nature does not mean, therefore, that he is determined by his organism. His body is creative. It has the power to go beyond itself and give birth to something that did not exist before.

This is what we call imagination. Man's body created for itself the possibility of leaving behind a past which had become dysfunctional and oppressive, thereby making it possible to act under the inspiration of his intentions. Man's body is an emi-

15. Alfred L. Kroeber and Talcott Parsons, "The Concepts of Culture and of Social System" (1958), p. 582.

grant: it moves out of the space where it has found itself, and which forced it into an adaptive course of behavior, and turns toward a new space still to be created. Man experiments with his space from the vantage point of the future. What can it become? Just as the pregnant woman looks at herself as someone who is going to be a mother, just as the artist sees his colors as possibilities of expression and communication, man looks at the world around him as raw material for a creative task to be carried out by the joint effort of heart and hands. As Pierre Furter puts its, for man "the goal is no longer to make sure that the space already conquered remains as it is, thereby eliminating the risks of temporality, but rather to temporalize the space. I become aware that the space where I live will be shaped by what I do. If the space tells me that the universe preexists my discovery of it, the temporalization of the space proves that this created universe is still unfinished."[16]

Behaviorism succeeded in demonstrating that man may behave like animals. If he is put in a situation from which all creative possibilities are eliminated—something like the Skinner box—under proper stimuli of pain and pleasure he is forced to pursue the adaptive course of action. For this to happen, however, his environment must have the same undeniable factualness, the same finality as it has for animals—so that he will learn, before everything else, that the global transformation of his situation is impossible. The game is there. He cannot refuse to play it. He cannot change the rules. If there is no way out he will learn the "right answers." And he will eventually love "Big Brother."

For this "theoretical breakthrough" to be achieved, however, man had to be taken away from the meaningful world where creativity is still possible. If the culture-creating act is made

16. *Educação e Vida* (1968), p. 26. My translation.

impossible, man will follow the logic of pain and pleasure. It is quite revealing, on the other hand, that he has a fantastic power to resist pain if he goes on believing in his values, i.e., if he preserves hope of the creative act. If man keeps on hoping, he will be able to remain whole in concentration camps, in exile, in captivity and slavery, in prisons and ghettos. In the torture chamber man succumbs not only because of pain, but because of the absolute hopelessness and helplessness of his situation. As Lecky pointed out, what threatens personality is not pain itself but the breakdown of the scheme of understanding and prediction.[17]

Thus there is something peculiar about man's body. The animal cannot help it: pain produces avoidance. It looks for a place in its environment where it need no longer suffer. In man, the logic of life is different. His body feels pain, but instead of simply avoiding it he asks whether it is not possible to transform the environment. And thus a process of pregnancy is started. Suffering triggers imagination, it gives birth to aspirations and expectations. And it ultimately gives shape to human behavior. As opposed to animals, which react only to the stimuli of their environment, man acts out of a passion for the absent—for what is lacking. Man wants to create values. His intention is to transform into reality what exists only in his imagination.

Thus, although both man and animals have bodies, they bring into being different temporalities and different worlds. The animal repeats the past in the present and moves towards the future in the same manner. Man, on the contrary, lives for the sake of the future he envisages, and his action in the present, instead of being a bare repetition of the past, is an act that aims at new creation. "An animal's actions are concerned with its

17. Prescott Lecky, *Self-Consistency: A Theory of Personality* (1961), p. 84.

future and the future of its young," remarks Buber, "but only man imagines the future: the beaver's dam is extended in a time-realm, but the planted tree is rooted in the world of time, and he who plants the first tree is he who will expect the Messiah."[18]

When we discover that we are both expecting the same Messiah, community is born. Until you reveal to me the hopes that activate your hands, I cannot love you. Maybe you hate what I love! How can we walk together if our hearts are set on different values? Maybe you want to abort my child, maybe I want to destroy yours. When we discover, however, that we share similar hopes, that we participate in the same symphony of groans, willing to risk our lives for the creation of a world we both love, we may clasp hands, embrace, and kiss each other. It is participation in a common universe of meaning that makes communication possible. *Community requires alliance of the spirit.* It cannot exist apart from the sense of ultimate commitment to a common future. And how beautiful it is when this discovery takes place! Words become unnecessary. Even silence communicates. Because in our silence our eyes and hearts are set on a common horizon. Love which takes place only in the immediacy of the present is a lie; it cannot endure. This is one of the great falsities of the traditional idea of Christian love. And this is the drama of the pastor who desperately struggles to keep his congregation together. He discovers that the price of this nice fellowship is avoidance of the critical issues that actually and unavoidably separate men from each other. People remain together to the extent that they hide from each other the real values to which they are committed. The price of fellowship which does not grow out of a true alliance of the heart is hypocrisy. This is one of the dramas of ecumenism. It wants to create

18. Martin Buber, *The Knowledge of Man* (1965), p. 62.

unity by institutional gimmicks—overlooking the fact that community has to grow out of life.

This is what lies beneath the dissolution of the nuclear family. There was a time when the family was both a functional unit and a community. Father, mother, and children performed certain tasks within a common universe of values. This universe fell apart. The father may go on making a living. The mother may still perform the tasks of a housewife. And the children may still do what they are "supposed to do." But even if the unit continues to function, it has lost its spirit. There is no longer common ground for communication, because its members have their loyalties turned toward opposite horizons. And this is a micro-example of what is taking place in the macro-sphere of society. The incredible degree of rationality and functionalism it has achieved cannot heal the radical splits that have divided it. Our values no longer coincide with the built-in tendencies of the social system. Although we still do our jobs, there is no way of avoiding the terrible sense of loss and meaninglessness, because our hearts are set on different values.

Community has a spiritual dimension. The fact that two of us perform similar functions in society does not mean at all that we can be friends. There is a religious element in this: the miracle of dialogue, the miracle of communication, the miracle of love are only born out of a common infinite passion for the absent that we both hide in our hearts and want to create with our hands. Durkheim perceived this fact with great clarity. "A society," he remarked, "is not made up merely of the mass of individuals who compose it, the ground which they occupy, the things which they use and the movements that they perform, but above all is the idea which it forms of itself."[19] And what is it that makes up this "idea"? It is the "dreams," the "aspira-

19. Émile Durkheim, *The Elementary Form of Religious Life* (1969) pp. 468–70.

tions," the "values," all of religious significance to the extent that they represent our highest hopes and have been born out of our common sufferings. It is the "hopes, yearnings, and purposes" of a group that reveal to us what it is, remarks Mannheim. The spirit of a community is its "dominant wish," the utopia it has generated and from which it lives.[20]

We find ourselves back in the biblical world. What is the community of faith? What is its distinctive element? All the categories based on social functions, on division of labor, on social stratification are brushed aside. The community of faith is not to be defined in terms of how it *reacts* to environmental *stimuli*. Its identity comes from the fact that it has tasted the *aperitif* of the future. It has visions of something that is as yet absent. And this that is absent is like a child slowly growing in the womb. The community suffers. But instead of trying to find a pleasant place in the geography of pain and pleasure, it accepts suffering as the pangs of childbirth. A creative act is needed, and this is what its life is all about. This is why its spirit can be discerned in the prayer which is hidden in all its groanings (cf. Rom. 8:18–28): "Thy Kingdom come, creation must be recreated, the present order of things must be abolished."

Let us return to the little prince. He had in his small asteroid a rose which he loved very much. How disappointed he was when he entered a garden on this earth, all abloom with roses! "And he was overcome with sadness. His flower had told him that she was the only one of her kind in all the universe. And here were five thousand of them, all alike, in one single garden!" But then he learned from the fox, that "what is essential is invisible to the eye." More importantly, he learned that it was the time he had wasted for his rose that made her so special. And he returned to the five thousand, saying, "You are not at

20. Karl Mannheim, *Ideology and Utopia* (1936), p. 188.

all like my rose. As yet you are nothing. No one has tamed you, and you have tamed no one. You are like my fox when I first knew him. He was a fox like a hundred thousand other foxes. But I have made him my friend, and now he is unique in all the world."[21]

The roses were all alike. But in truth they were not. Between the little prince and his rose was something that made all the difference in the world. They belonged to each other in a way in which he did not belong to the other roses. The values we hide in our hearts are what matter. We are all bodies—the differences between us are negligible. But each has something unique. Each body hides a heart, a vision, a love, tears and joys. How could one truly experience the other's body without having first loved what the other loves? I may touch you, you may touch me. These are physical stimuli which can be pleasant or unpleasant, just as with mice in laboratories. But to the extent that simple "body awareness" or "body sensitivity" goes on, the secret remains hidden—and with it the meaning of the body. The body is an arrow. You must see it flying. You must hear its voice, it must reveal its hidden destination. It is only then that we discover whether we are companions on a common journey or enemies filled with poison. Could you kiss a snake? Or make love with a scorpion? Tell me what you love, and then I can embrace you. How could it be otherwise?

Why am I saying all this? To remind the reader that, once we create values and hopes, once our imagination and our hands build the meaningful cosmos we call culture, we can no longer go back to the body and to nature. The body is not merely a sensitive device. We do not know it just by touching and hugging and kissing. The human body is creative. It gives birth to values. What it creates belongs to it in a much more intense

21. Saint–Exupéry, *op. cit.*, pp. 77, 86–87.

form even than its limbs. I can lose a leg or an arm and still my values are preserved. No one is truly related to the body if he is not related to its dearest child. Thus culture starts with the body, but transfigures it—more precisely, the body transfigures itself. And once it engenders hopes and aspirations, they become extensions of it, and the body ceases to experience life through the immediacy of the senses and begins to feel it through the mediation of the heart. Our eyes, our ears, our skin, our tongue—they know life according to the values the heart cherishes. The music that makes me laugh or cry, the food that gives me pleasure or indigestion, the touch that brings me joy or distress—are all related to my cultural roots, my aspirations, and those specific ways of feeling life which are peculiar to the culture to which I belong. Strictly identical sensorial experiences can have totally different meanings. Perhaps this is nowhere more evident than in the sphere of sex, one of the most powerful of our biological drives. Yet we experience it through the mediation of our values. As Masters and Johnson show, many people who have perfect bodies cannot enjoy sex because of cultural attitudes.[22]

The same may be said of nature. We never experience it as a mere fact, a simple bundle of stimuli. We see it through the mediation of the heart. This is true of the most primitive man as of the most objective-minded scientist. Our culture may lead us to contemplate nature with awe and respect, or to consider it as nothing more than raw material for economic organization and therefore something to be plundered and ravaged.

Culture becomes the body of man. The intention of the magician, the desires of the child, the dreams of the utopian become flesh. The heart triumphs over "reality." The reasons of the heart succeed in creating a new Reality, an environment which

22. W. H. Masters and V. E. Johnson, *Human Sexual Inadequacy* (1970).

is both instrumental for and expressive of its aspirations. The power of love opens a new space for the game of life to go on in. Imagination delivers its child.

Culture becomes Reality for man. It abolishes the alien and inhuman order of power, whether natural or political, and transfigures it. Both body and nature are resurrected in a new form which grows out of the heart. Imagination gives birth to a new creation. And "In the beginning was the Body" becomes "In the beginning was the Word"—so that man can say, "In the end will be Life."

Berdyaev once remarked that "magic will be creative and active and will remove the spell from nature and lead it out of its torpidity."[23] In culture, the intention of the magician is fulfilled. The once painful confession that "reality is not moved by man's wishes" is overcome by the creative act that reshapes it according to the heart's desire.

Play proclaims that the order of life should not be controlled by the imposition of an alien power. It expresses the yearning for a new form of social organization which will deliver pleasure instead of pain, which will express freedom instead of coercion. In culture, play becomes politics. Now life "indulges in manifestations with no purpose or utility of any sort, for the mere pleasure of affirming itself."[24]

And the dream of the utopian ceases to be a dream. Its longing becomes history.

Has the unfinished experiment come to an end?

Has the perpetual emigrant found a permanent home?

Has the wild duck finally decided to beat its wings no longer?

Has the rebel at last become adjusted?

No. The culture-creating act is no more than a sabbath: a resting place in an unending journey. It is an *aperitif* which

23. Nikolai Berdyaev, *The Meaning of the Creative Act* (1955), p. 319.
24. Durkheim, *op. cit.*, p. 471.

always says there is still something to come. Have you ever tried to reach the horizon? Every horizon denies itself, for there is always a beyond. Life is never exhausted. There are new possibilities ahead, new occasions for joy, new pregnancies to be conceived.

So is there no end?

This really should not be the question. The question is whether a situation will ever exist in which a new beginning is impossible. And what I am saying is that, because of imagination, life can always begin again. Culture has become our body. This gives us the incredible freedom to die. Our cultural body can be dissolved—without bringing life to an end. On the contrary, through dying life can start again. Death and resurrection can take place. Man is free to give up the long-held presuppositions of what was once a meaningful culture, which has become old and senile with time. And as he does so, he discovers that beyond death and dissolution the creative act is possible once more. And he is free to go on exploring the infinite possibilities of the unfinished experiment which is his own life.

Part 3

Imagination
and the Conception of the Future

Alas, where shall I climb with my longing? From all mountains I look out for fatherlands and motherlands. But home is found nowhere; a fugitive am I in all cities and a departure at all gates. Strange and a mockery to me are the men of today to whom my heart recently drew me; I am driven out of fatherlands and motherlands. Thus I now love only my children's land, yet undiscovered, in the farthest sea: for this I bid my sails search and search.

—FRIEDRICH NIETZSCHE

Sing aloud, O barren woman who never bore a child, break into cries of joy, you who have never been in labour; for the deserted wife has more sons than she who lives in wedlock. . . .

—ISAIAH 54:1

11

The Seed of the Future: The Community of Hope

I belong to a frustrated generation and it is out of this experience that I think and speak.

I have learned that it is useless to speak to people in general. Our ability to understand does not go beyond the limits of our experience. Very few words are needed when we have eaten of the same bread, and a multiplicity of words is of no avail if we have not felt common sufferings and hopes. Even strange words draw us together when they come from a common experience, whereas common words divide us when they express opposite life experiences. Understanding is a miracle which grows out of an unspoken secret: the common paths trodden by individuals who nevertheless have never met and will never meet.

The Brazilian poet Vinicius de Moraes says that "ninguem pode ser universal fora do seu quintal"—nobody can be universal away from his own back yard. My story is my back yard. And this is the bread I share with those who have pursued a similar path. Everything I have said in the foregoing chapters is an attempt to put together the jigsaw puzzle of my life.

Where did our journey begin? We started with those beautiful visions which immediately followed World War II. It never entered our minds that that war could be the symptom of an incurable disease which infected both victors and vanquished. We felt it to be something like a satanic invasion, something not programed, an abnormality, a wave of diabolical forces trying to destroy the slowly building paradise in which we were all involved. The end of the war was like the victory of heaven over hell, of good over evil, of truth over falsehood, of Christ over the anti-Christ. The demons were expelled, chaos was pushed back, and the miracle of Creation took place again. The end of the war made it possible for us to resurrect the world view of liberalism and the dreams and hopes that the nineteenth century had produced. From then on, so we believed, a new future lay ahead, open and promising. Peace had finally triumphed, and reason could resume the interrupted task of building the earth through its handmaids, science and technology.

But our hopes were shortlived. The cold war, the insanity of the arms race, political and economic imperialism, the growing gap between rich and poor nations, the realities of hunger, exploitation, and oppression—all proclaimed the sickness of our civilization. We hoped to build a tower with its top reaching to heaven, but were left only with confusion and frustration. The evil spirits of the concentration camps had not been expelled; they still wandered in our spaces and haunted our times. Hungary and Santo Domingo, Czechoslovakia and Vietnam—they were the end of the liberal dream.

It became obvious that the world needed a radical transformation. We could no longer move toward the future as though there were nothing basically wrong in our civilization. Out of this vision revolutionary hopes and movements were born. Politics became the new religion, and religion became politics.

Christians discovered a new meaning for their faith. From all quarters a new prophetic message began to be heard: "Already the axe is laid to the roots of the trees. The hour of judgment has come. Repent and be transformed." No longer the opiate of the people, religion became suddenly an instrument of liberation. Perhaps the Church could be transformed into a revolutionary community! Perhaps the hour was at hand for her to become the midwife of a new future for mankind. And those who had exchanged their religious faith for a political ideology lived their ideologies with true religious fervor and found in their action groups the communal and messianic meaning they longed for.

Again hopes were followed by frustration. Voices from the past had already warned us that there was something wrong in the naïve identification of revolution with liberation. With bitter sadness Berdyaev had warned, "It is an illusion that revolution breaks with the old. It is only that the old makes its appearance with a new mask on. The old slavery changes its dress, the old inequality is transformed into a new inequality."[1] Martin Buber had likewise suggested that "as regards their positive goal revolutions will always result in the exact opposite of what the most honest and passionate revolutionaries strive for, unless and until this has so far taken shape before the revolution."[2] But there was no time to waste. One could not stop for provisos, "unless and until." The clatter of slogans is always more convincing than the whisper of the prophets. Nobody paid any attention to them. The revolutionaries' hopes became dogmas —and dogmas are evil spirits which make us blind.

Revolutionaries believed it was enough to destroy the old. What shape was the new society to take? How was the new space and time created by the act of dissolution to be orga-

1. Nikolai Berdyaev, *Slavery and Freedom* (1944), p. 196.
2. Martin Buber, *Paths in Utopia* (1958), p. 44.

nized? These questions did not disturb them. History was on their side; history itself was bringing the old society to an end. Their task was simply to join history in passing final judgment on the old order. As to the future, history would take care of it. Beyond the negative act of dissolution a new society and a new man would automatically be created by the very forces that were now shaking our foundations. Beyond the iron determinism of material dialectics, they proclaimed, mankind would find freedom. They never stopped to think that "freedom which is a result of necessity cannot be real freedom; it is only an element in the dialectic of necessity."[3]

They did not perceive that any act which is solely concerned with negation is self-defeating. Negation aims at dissolving the action initiated by the oppressor. The Master establishes a frontier of oppression. By organizing itself in response to the dominant structure of power the revolutionary preserves, as if in a photographic negative, the very shape of the power it wants to abolish. *Whenever action is reaction, it is bound to be reactionary.* This is why it is sheer stupidity to repay evil with evil. Reaction is bad tactics. It frustrates the fundamental intention. Even when evil is defeated, it triumphs to the extent that it remains the only creative factor in the situation. According to Nietzsche, this is the fateful mistake of slave morality. "The slaves' revolt in morals begins with this, that *ressentiment* itself becomes creative and gives birth to values. Whereas all noble morality grows out of a triumphant affirmation of oneself, slave morality immediately says No to what comes from outside, to what is different, to what is not oneself: and this No is its creative deed. It requires external stimuli in order to react at all: its action is at bottom always reaction."[4] That was the tragedy of

3. Berdyaev, *op. cit.*, p. 60.
4. Friedrich Nietzsche, *Toward a Genealogy of Morals*, in Walter Kaufmann, ed., *The Portable Nietzsche* (1968), p. 451.

revolution: it lacked the positive vision of a new future for mankind.

There is no historical evidence to support the belief that freedom follows naturally upon the act of dissolution. "To imagine and believe that the revolutionary act will inaugurate a radically new time implies a magical attitude which does not satisfy the canons of a rigorous reflection, and which is dangerous for a responsible political action."[5] This is a survival, in the consciousness of the revolutionary, of his religious origins, and an expression of his craving for religious shortcuts. As pious people used to say that one need not worry about the future because God is in charge, the revolutionary says the same because history is in charge.

Negation may expel an evil spirit, but it cannot create a positive reality. "When an unclean spirit comes out of a man it wanders over the deserts seeking a resting-place; and if it finds none, it says, 'I will go back to the home I left.' So it returns and finds the house swept clean, and tidy. Off it goes and collects seven other spirits more wicked than itself, and they all come in and settle down; and in the end the man's plight is worse than before" (Luke 11:24–26).

For lack of a positive vision, the tactics of negation condemns itself to repeat in another form what was negated. No wonder similar organization trends follow the coups of the right and revolutions of the left; they exhibit identical symptoms. The economy has to be rationalized, so that production and consumption are properly interlocked. Power becomes Organization, and dysfunctional elements must be brought under control. Both, it appears, are trying to make the same pudding, though they disagree as to the recipe.

But our frustration cannot be explained only by the self-

5. Pierre Furter, *L'Imagination Créatrice, La Violence et le Changement Social* (1968), p. 3/7. My translation.

defeating tendency of the tactics of negation. The other factor
is that, thanks to science, power now manages to organize itself
so as to be very nearly invulnerable. The negators of power look
like Don Quixote confronting his windmills. For the present, at
least, one can no longer maintain any hope of overthrowing the
dominant powers, as I tried to show in the first section of this
book.

The signs of the times are unequivocal. The dynamic of
creativity has been banned from politics. The love of power
manages to control the power of love. The result is that we live
in a world in which, in the words of Paul Goodman, "the means
lack goods and the goods lack means."[6] Those who have imagination do not have power, whereas those who have power do
not have imagination. "The higher values in the world appear
to be weaker than the lower, the higher values are crucified, the
lower triumph. The politician and the sergeant major, the
banker and the lawyer, are stronger than the poet and the
philosopher, the prophet and the saint. The Son of God was
crucified. Socrates was poisoned. The prophets were stoned.
The initiators and creators of a new thought and a new way of
living have always been persecuted, and oppressed and often
put to death."[7]

It is true that this state of affairs is not peculiar to our times.
The alienation of power is perhaps the most persistent tendency of civilization: its original sin. Its roots are deep down in
the existential situation of man, his anxieties and fear of freedom. In the past, however, there have been critical moments
in which the heart was able to overthrow the power that repressed it, thus making it possible for life to create a new body
for itself. This situation has drastically changed. Science and
technology have put too much power in the hands of the power-

6. Paul Goodman, *Utopian Essays and Practical Proposals* (1962), p 12.
7. Berdyaev, *op. cit.*, p. 67.

ful. No matter how hard life struggles to be free, it seems that the structures of domination are always stronger.

We have undergone a monstrous surgical operation. Organization has managed to separate the order of efficiency from the order of the heart—science from the concrete longings of mankind—hands from aspirations. The culture-creating act has thus been made impossible; for, as we have seen, culture implies a synthesis of these two orders in such a way that the order of effectiveness functions as a tool and means of expression of the order of the heart. By this separation the very presuppositions of human wholeness have been destroyed. Our world abounds in power but is devoid of meaning.

Nowhere in our civilization do we see the creative act taking place. As a result, we do not know what battles to fight. Every effort seems useless. We no longer have any sense of direction. Unamuno once remarked that we *are* the battles that we fight. "Pugno, ergo sum." When we come to the conclusion that no battle is worth fighting, a dangerous process of internal dissolution begins to take place. The self loses its center, and with it the sense that life is worth living.

This generation once believed that we were at a turning point in history, that a new world was being born. We felt like pilgrims in the Exodus on our way to the Promised Land. Today we feel that the reality is quite the opposite. We are exiles in a Captivity, and it is unlikely that we shall ever see the Promised Land. This is the source of our frustration. What shall we do about it?

As I have already suggested, the pain of frustration can be removed by adaptation. If one is too fat to fly, why go on ludicrously flapping one's wings? It is easier to put on the identity of the domestic duck. And in so doing one comes to believe that this is the best of all possible worlds and there is nothing basically wrong with it. For all practical purposes, the Messiah has arrived. His glory fills the whole earth. One lives in an atmosphere of realized eschatology; one experiences the pleasant feeling of being *reconciled* with reality. All the social contradictions have been or will shortly be solved by the power of the dominant order of things.

Another possibility is simply to accept frustration in an attitude of resignation. Despairing of their dreams, revolutionaries come to the bitter conclusion that there is no hope for history. This is the mood one finds over and over again in the writings of the old Niebuhr. "The liberal world manages to achieve a tolerable life in a kind of confusion of purposes," he says, "which is better than the organization of the whole resources of a community for the achievement of false ends." There is a profound pessimism here. The best that can be achieved is "a tolerable life in a kind of confusion of purposes."[8] The possibility of organizing the whole resources of a community for the achievement of true ends is not even mentioned. Social creativity is dismissed as either a utopian dream or an ideological demon, with its ultimate roots in man's selfishness and self-deception. The hopes of the past are identified with illusions. And if one's hopes are illusions, so are one's frustrations—ultimately "healthy" experiences which bring us back to reality. And frustration is displaced by resignation.

But suppose one decides not to give up one's hopes and aspirations. In the past saints have built monasteries, visionaries founded esoteric sects, and men of all kinds have been convinced that their values were flowers too delicate to grow in the human desert among the stones, cactus, scorpions, and snakes. The world is evil. How can love blossom in it? So with infinite patience they built greenhouses where they planted the seeds of their hopes. Away and apart from the world—this is the space

8. Reinhold Niebuhr, *Christian Realism and Political Problems* (1953), pp. 5–6.

and the time where the Messiah comes. Away and apart from the world—this is where human life can be truly human.

Here is the gospel of the counter-culture. It takes up with infinite care the values the world has vomited forth, and plants them within the commune. "See!" it says. "The future has already arrived. It is in our midst. The experience of fullness is not a distant hope to be realized in a world which refuses to be redeemed. It is real in the immediacy of our present. Eat and drink! Enjoy play, celebration, drugs, sex, mystical experiences, wonder—these are the sacraments of the divine! The time for sublimation is past. The age of enjoyment has arrived."

The counter-culture's fight against sublimation is a struggle against Organization, because this has been the most widely used mechanism in transforming the body into a function of the system. But the most profound of all the intentions of the human body is the will to be creative. It does not find happiness by simply having pleasant sense experiences. It wants to become pregnant and give birth to a friendly world. Creativity is the way out of the logic of the dinosaur—it is the logic of life itself. This is what I have tried to show in the second section of the present volume. And it is what this frustrated generation wanted to accomplish through political action.

And its intention was aborted, and people were left with a problem: the erotic build-up that resulted from the expectation that the right time for conception had arrived. Now that intercourse and pregnancy are ruled out—what to do with all the emotions that wanted to become creativity? *The creative intention is resolved by being sublimated in sense-derived and immediate sense experiences.* The will to make pregnant is dissolved by means of masturbation: dancing, celebration, mystical visions—pleasure-producing experiences which do not fertilize anything. One is content with a "substitute-gratification." When counter-culture proclaims that the Messiah has already arrived in the commune, when it announces that politics is no longer necessary and that the time of creativity is past and the eternal "sabbath" has arrived, it does not see how deeply committed it is to sublimation. Its proclaimed rebellious style of life actually functions as the opiate of the people. The body has despaired of itself. It no longer believes in its power to transform the earth, and resolves its frustration by becoming intoxicated with the present. Thus, by providing the orgiastic, mystical, and philosophical means for the sublimation of creativity, counter-culture transforms otherwise dysfunctional body impulses into styles of life which are functional to the very Organization it hates.

Thus runs the script of our frustration.

The politics of liberalism turned out to be the logic of the dinosaur. The politics of revolution was trapped in its self-defeating tendencies even before it was reduced to impotence by the power of Organization. And the politics of counter-culture despaired of the possibility of being creative.

Bonhoeffer perceived very well our tragic predicament. "Surely there has never been a generation in the course of human history with so little ground under its feet as our own," he remarked. "Every conceivable alternative seems equally intolerable."[9] How can we become adapted to captivity, or exchange our hopes for resignation? How can we behave *as if* the world were free, and dance and play and celebrate *as if* we were not exiles?

Alas, we must learn to sing the song of the exile.

> By the waters of Babylon we sat down and wept
>   when we remembered Zion.
> There on the willow-trees
>   we hung up our harps,

9. Dietrich Bonhoeffer, *Letters and Papers from Prison* (1953), pp. 13–14.

> for there those who carried us off
>   demanded music and singing,
> and our captors called on us to be merry:
>   'Sing us one of the songs of Zion.'
> How could we sing the Lord's song
>   in a foreign land?
>
> If I forget you, O Jerusalem,
>   let my right hand wither away;
> let my tongue cling to the roof of my mouth
>   if I do not remember you,
> if I do not set Jerusalem
>   above my highest joy.
>   . . . .
> O Babylon, Babylon the destroyer,
>   happy the man who repays you
>   for all that you did to us!
> Happy is he who shall seize your children
>   and dash them against the rock. [Psalm 137]

It is no wonder that out of this bitterness revolutionary dreams and leaders naturally emerged. The hope was a single one: to go back home again. But for the escape to take place, the walls of the prison had to be destroyed.

Right in the midst of these dreams, a strange letter from Jeremiah arrived with a fatal blow to their plans.

These are the words of the Lord of Hosts the God of Israel: To all the exiles whom I have carried off from Jerusalem to Babylon: Build houses and live in them; plant gardens and eat their produce. Marry wives and beget sons and daughters; take wives for your sons and give your daughters to husbands, so that they may bear sons and daughters and you may increase there and not dwindle away. [Jer. 29:4–7]

How unbearable these words must have sounded. To wait for the fruits of the trees they were to plant, to live in the knowledge that even their grandchildren would still be in captivity, this was too much for anyone whose patience did not exceed the six months which elapse between the planting of the pumpkin and the eating of the pie. "When a full seventy years has passed over Babylon, I will take up your cause. . . . says the Lord." Forget about liberation in your lifetime. You will never see Jerusalem again.

Jeremiah was cursed as a traitor and damned as a reactionary. However, a strange thing took place just then. Jerusalem was under siege. No hope of deliverance could be realistically maintained. In this moment, when no one of sound mind could make any plans for the future, Jeremiah bought a piece of land. What a bad investment! Obviously— Yet the purpose of his action was not economic but symbolic and prophetic. Only a man ultimately committed to and convinced of his hopes would do something like that. "The time will come when houses, fields, and vineyards will again be bought and sold in this land," he announced (Jer. 32:15). What a strange person he is! He rejects both the revolutionaries' illusions of quick delivery and the despair that no longer sees any future. He becomes neither a prophet of revolution nor a priest of the status quo, nor yet a guru who carries out the ceremonials that sublimate creativity. In captivity he keeps his hope alive.

Why is it so important to go on hoping? Because without hope one will be either dissolved in the existing state of things or devoured by insanity. Even psychiatric therapy has already recognized that without hope human wholeness is not possible. Personality is able to preserve its values in a situation that contradicts them only to the extent that it believes the future will vindicate its expectations. The case of a patient without hope is, in fact, hopeless.[10]

10. Ezra Stotland, *The Psychology of Hope* (1969).

What is hope?

It is the *presentiment* that *imagination is more real* and *reality less real than it looks*. It is the *hunch* that the overwhelming brutality of facts that oppress and repress is not the last word. It is the *suspicion* that Reality is much more complex than realism wants us to believe; that the frontiers of the possible are not determined by the limits of the actual, and that in a miraculous and unexpected way life is preparing the creative event which will open the way to freedom and resurrection.

Perhaps one of the most intriguing descriptions of hope we find in the Bible is the story of Abraham and Sarah. They had built their whole lives around the obsessive desire for a child. Facts, however, did not meet their expectations; Abraham and Sarah grew old, and the child did not come. "Hope seemed hopeless." However, "without any weakening of faith, he contemplated his own body, *as good as dead* (for he was about a hundred years old), and *the deadness of Sarah's womb,*" for he believed in the God "who makes the dead live and summons things that are not yet in existence as if they already were" (Rom. 4:17–19—emphasis supplied).

Or take Habakkuk's prayer.

> Although the fig-tree does not burgeon,
> the vines bear no fruit,
> · the olive-crop fails,
> the orchards yield no food,
> the fold is bereft of its flock
> and there are no cattle in the stalls,
> *yet* I will exult in the Lord
> and rejoice in the God of my deliverance.
> [Hab. 3:17—emphasis supplied]

The facts have already passed their verdict on the desires of the heart. They are defeated. *Yet*—this is the word that makes all the difference—one moves toward the future in the certainty that the present has not said all that is to be said. And one literally bets one's life on this coming but still unseen creative event. It seems to me that this is what faith in God is all about. It is not the knowledge that there is a Being who lives somewhere in or outside this universe. For the Bible, to believe in God is the same as to believe that, contrary to our realistic assessment of the situation, something new and unexpected will suddenly erupt, thus changing completely the possibilities of human life and fulfillment.

There is no universal recipe for living. Living has to do with a choice of contexts. It is up to us to choose the relevant points of reference—the horizons—the directions—or, if you will, the stimuli which are going to make up the world to which we are responsible. Living is like dancing. As you dance you move your body according to a rhythm and a harmony which fill the space. The complexity of our human predicament is due to the fact that a number of conflicting rhythms and harmonies are being played at the same time. You cannot dance them all; if you try, you become schizophrenic and your body is split (or immobilized) by contradictory dynamics. Personality demands integration. As Kierkegaard once said that purity of heart is to will one thing only, so we might say that purity of heart is to dance to one rhythm only.

You may dance the tune played by the present reality. Your style of life will be realistic and pragmatic. Or you may choose to move your body under the spell of a mysterious tune and rhythm which come from a world we do not see, the world of our hopes and aspirations. *Hope is hearing the melody of the future. Faith is to dance it.* You risk your life, and you take your risk to its ultimate conclusion, even the cross, because you detect a strange odor of death mixed with the fascinating music of Mephisto, lord of the "present evil world." The rhythms of the future, on the other hand, contain promises of freedom, love, and life. It is worth the risk—even if we lose!

What is it that makes us hope? Our desires? Hardly. For it is so common that desires become illusions. In the biblical world, *one hopes for the future because one has already seen the creative event taking place in the past.* The prophets looked to the past because it provided the clues that enabled them to see the form the creative event was taking in their present. "Memory" added something to the eyes, made it possible to "discern the signs of the times." Our bewilderment is due to the fact that the criteria by which we used to analyze our human condition no longer work. We apply the stethoscope to the womb of our historical moment in the hope that we will hear the heartbeat of a child, and we do not hear anything. This does not necessarily mean that there is no creative event in process, but rather that something may be wrong with our stethoscope. We are bewildered because, as Bonhoeffer pointed out, we stand at a turning point of history where the new which is being formed is "not discernible in the alternatives of the present."[11]

The problem of hope is that of finding out the shape the creative event takes in captivity. And here we go back to Jeremiah. His reading of history had told him that not all times are moments of exodus. As a woman cannot give birth if she has not become pregnant, so history cannot produce liberation if the conditions are not ripe for it. We must never forget the revolutionary event "is not so much a creative as a delivering force whose function is to set free and authenticate, i.e., it can only perfect, set free, and lend the stamp of authority to something that has already been foreshadowed in the womb of the pre-revolutionary society; the hour of revolution is not an hour of

11. *Op. cit.,* p. 14.

begetting but an hour of birth, provided there was a begetting beforehand."[12]

In the larger sense, captivity is not a time of birth. This is not, therefore, the form that the creative event could be taking in the present. But it can be a time of conception. If ours is not the harvest season, it may well be a time for sowing. Our soil looks "poor and domesticated." "No tall tree is able to grow in it."[13] But this does not matter. In spite—and because—of the fact that our tall trees have been cut down, our air polluted with fear, and our soil turned into a heap of refuse, a new seed must be planted: the seed of our highest hope.

This is the political task now possible.

If our child cannot be born in this time, we can at least make of our present the moment of conception. In the words of Buber, our task is to "create here and now the space *now* possible for the thing that we are striving for, so that it may come to fulfilment *then*."[14]

How to start the creative act? What shall we do?

There is no answer to these questions. The Bible does not know anything about the mechanics of conception and birth of a creative event. The simple fact that creativity implies the abandonment of the life presuppositions that have gone before indicates that it cannot be explained as the *result* of an earlier *cause*. "The wind blows where it wills; you hear the sound of it, but you do not know where it comes from, or where it is going. So with everyone who is born from spirit" (John 3:8). "The creative act," Jung once remarked, "will forever elude the human understanding."[15]

The Bible does not tell *how* it happens but *that* it happens.

12. Buber, *op. cit.*, pp. 44–45.
13. Friedrich Nietzsche, *Thus Spoke Zarathustra*, in Kaufmann, ed., *op. cit.*, p. 129.
14. *Op. cit.*, p. 13.
15. Quoted in Harold Rugg, *Imagination* (1963), p. 3.

It seems to me that this is what the "sociology of liberation" that is articulated through the biblical symbols, myths, and stories is all about. It does not explain; it describes. It does not provide recipes, but it points to the *signs* or the *fruits* of the Spirit. In traditional theological language, we are not saved by works: *we cannot produce the creative event.* We are saved by grace. The creative event simply takes place and offers itself to us, without our being able to provide an explanation for its genesis. The only thing that we can do is *to join it.*

The Bible answers the question as to the historical shape of the creative act by pointing to a community. The "community of faith" is that social reality where creativity is incarnated. It gains flesh and bones. In this community the future takes on space in the time still present: it is the "objectification of the Spirit," *the place where the creative insight and the creative intention become creative power.*

Our idealistic heritage exerts an influence upon us which is more pervasive than we want to admit. We tend to believe that the task of regeneration of culture and of the rebirth of civilization can be solved by means of intellectual insights. This is why so many books are still written in the attempt to discover the nature of the good. We still believe that we do wrong things because we do not know they are wrong. We operate under the illusion that the dinosaur can be convinced by means of arguments, and we forget that, by its logic, anything that does not increase its power is a priori ruled out as false and evil. The dinosaur has a quite sensitive stomach. Any potion which implies death and resurrection is immediately vomited and those who have prepared it devoured.

Insights in themselves are powerless. No matter how true, they are impotent to bring about change. Words and thoughts have no *ex opere operato* power. As Schiller pointed out, "When truth is to triumph in the struggle with force, it must itself first become a *force* and put up some *drive* as its advocate in the realm of phenomena; for drives are the only moving forces in the world of feeling."[16] In traditional theological language, the Word must become flesh: vision must become power if the world is to be redeemed. To the ethical question "What shall I do?" the Bible replies by pointing to the community where the logic of death and resurrection—or the logic of creativity—has assumed space and time and has determined the style and direction of human interrelatedness. It seems to me that Paul Lehmann is the only ethical thinker among our contemporaries who has perceived this fact with clarity. The question of the good is really the question of the *koinonia,* the community which embodies the messianic thrust of the creative intention.

The Bible puts us in a bewildering situation. It acknowledges that the creative event erupts in history and assumes a social form, but it does not have any formula for duplicating it. The community cannot be mass-produced. We have no recipe for programing its growth or proliferation. But then what are we to do? The New Testament simply says: "Believe the good news"—somewhere, somehow it is happening. "Repent": throw away your old stethoscope and find a way of hearing the heartbeat of the future already pulsating in a community. And "be baptized": join it.

Our task is thus simply to be able to recognize the social marks of the creative event. What is its physiognomy? How does it look?

The biblical answer is quite disturbing. Only the oppressed can be creative. Why? Because only the oppressed have the will to abolish the power presuppositions which are at the root of their oppression.

16. Quoted by Walter Kaufmann in *Hegel: A Reinterpretation* (1965), p. 31.

In no other place is this insight expressed with deeper pathos than in the song of the Suffering Servant (Isa. 53:1–12). This poem is an attempt to answer the same question we are raising now: How is it possible to go on hoping in captivity? What are the signs of hope in the midst of despair? What are the signs of the creative act, when creativity has become essentially an underground business? What is God up to in this situation? "To whom has the power of the Lord been revealed?" And then the answer follows:

> He grew up before the Lord like a young plant
> whose roots are in parched ground;
> he had no beauty, no majesty to draw our eyes,
> no grace to make us delight in him;
> his form, disfigured, lost all the likeness of a man,
> his beauty changed beyond human semblance.
> He was despised, he shrank from the sight of men,
> tormented and humbled by suffering. . . .
> Without protection, without justice, he was taken away. . . .

By identifying the Liberator with the Suffering Slave, the Bible affirms that the oppressed, and not the rich and powerful, are the seed of a new future. How difficult it is for the rich to enter the Kingdom. They inhabit the pleasure-producing zones of reality, and as a consequence cannot do anything but say with the false prophet, "All is well."

> But alas for you who are rich; you have had your time of happiness.
> Alas for you who are well-fed now; you shall go hungry.
> Alas for you who laugh now; you shall mourn and weep. [Luke 6:24–25]

Those who live in the pain-delivering sectors of our society, however, even before they can articulate in speech the evil of this world, are already doing it by means of their inarticulate groans (Rom. 8:26). And this is the raw material the Spirit takes unto Himself. In other words: this is the emotional matrix which is the beginning of the creative event.

Suffering prepares the soul for vision. Personality refuses to take things as they are. It spreads its wings and the heart emigrates to the horizons of the future. Imagination is born, and with it the ideal future that the community of suffering engenders out of its own existential situation. Every sigh of oppression contains a vision of the Kingdom which is to come.

If it were not for this vision the community would be entrapped in the tactics of negation. By itself, suffering can only produce bitterness, resentment, and the ethics of reaction. Suffering alone is not creative. It must first become pregnant, must give birth to hope. That springing up of hope is the moment when the community turns away from the ethics of resentment in order to become creative. It is the moment when one realizes that for the desert to become a garden it is not enough to pluck up thorns and thistles: one must plant flowers and orchards.

A new social reality is born. Resentment is displaced. Hope becomes the emotional matrix, the ultimate concern, the highest "idea" (Durkheim), the spirit of the community. "A mere possibility materializes and becomes real before it exists in fact."[17] Thus the community of hope is a partial realization of the dream of the utopian visionaries. For it is the future actually taking place in the present. The community is a "sample" of the "not yet," the *aperitif* of a banquet still to come.

It is a partial realization of the intention of play, because in the community of faith the form of human interrelatedness is not determined by the "present evil world" but rather by the vision that has grown out of common longings and aspirations. It is a sign of the possibility of a social order based on freedom. Clearly not a supermarket style of freedom. The Bible totally

17. Leszek Kolakowski, *Toward a Marxist Humanism* (1968), p. 36.

ignores this possibility of life. *Freedom is the will to creativity that a community embodies in itself. It is communal discipline for the sake of the future.*

And finally, just as the magician represented in his behavior the axiological priority of the pleasure principle over the reality principle, we have in this community the representation and reenactment of the common vision of a new future. The community of faith is thus the social form of imagination. "And Imagination became Flesh and dwelt among us and we saw its grace, truth, and promise."

What the biblical sociology of liberation tells through the symbol of the community is thus unequivocal: the creative event cuts its way through the social inertia by creating a *counter-culture.* In the Old Testament, the community of Israel was a counter-culture. Its life-style, values, and patterns of human interrelatedness were radically different from and opposed to the dominant cultural patterns of its environment. The early Christian community was a counter-culture. Or more precisely, an *underground* counter-culture. The reason it was so ruthlessly persecuted was because the dominant powers perceived it as a basically dysfunctional and subversive social reality. The values it wanted to realize and live out implied in the long run the abolition of the very foundations of the Roman Empire.

"If this is the case," one might ask, "why have you such deep reservations against the present counter-culture phenomenon?"

If a woman wants to get pregnant, she had better stop taking the pill. This, for me, is the paradox of counter-culture. It wants to create and give birth to new values. But its political practice is like a contraceptive device which will render its creative insights sterile. In *Paradise Lost* Milton says that "the mind is its own place, and in itself can make a Heaven of Hell, a Hell of Heaven." This is the metaphysics and social theory of the politics of consciousness. But captivity is not abolished by wishing it away. The slave's dreams of liberation do not break his chains. When one lives *as if* one were free, one no longer needs to prepare for the creative act. Man ceases to be an arrow. He becomes like the last man described by Nietzsche, who found happiness and became unable to give birth to a star.

Yes, the new values, sacraments of the future, must be lived in the present. One must play, celebrate, dance, experience wonder, rediscover the body. But what if one gets intoxicated by the *aperitif?* What if one gets fat just by eating the sample? The wild duck will never fly again, and the wanderers in the desert will settle for the fleshpots of Egypt. If dancing, play, celebration, and wonder become substitute-gratifications they will sublimate the creative intention of the community. For creation to take place, suffering and hope cannot be separated. Suffering is the thorn that makes it impossible for us to forget that there is a political task still unfinished—still to be accomplished. And hope is the star that tells the direction to follow. The two, suffering and hope, live from each other. Suffering without hope produces resentment and despair. Hope without suffering creates illusions, naïveté, and drunkenness.

The experience of pleasure and joy should make us even more aware that the world is not really open to pleasure and joy. The air all around us is filled with sorrow and pain. How can love close its ears to this, and plunge itself into the oblivion of immediate experience? Love looks for effectiveness. Love demands power. The gifts of the future enjoyed in community must function like the preliminaries of love: they must create the excitement that prepares one for the great experience still to come. They are its *sacrament,* the *aperitif* of the absent, of the possible, of that which does not yet exist. And therefore they contain *the ethical and political imperative of creative love.*

If you keep in mind that a counter-culture, by implying a

redefinition of the game of life, must always look like madness, you will see that Paul in this text is speaking of the counter-culture character of the community of faith, and of the unavoidable political imperative that belongs to it.

Divine folly is wiser than the wisdom of man, and divine weakness stronger than man's strength. My brothers, think what sort of people you are, whom God has called. Few of you are men of wisdom, by any human standard; few are powerful or highly born. Yet [that magic word!] to shame the wise, God has chosen what the world counts folly, and to shame what is strong, God has chosen what the world counts weakness. He has chosen things low and contemptible, mere nothings to overthrow the existing order. [1 Cor. 1:25–29]

This is not the moment of birth. It is not the moment of political confrontation. But if we are sowing something really new, it is inevitable that the community of faith and the existing order are on collision course. Persecution will come.

It is time to stop planting pumpkins.

Let us plant dates, even though those who plant them will never eat them.

If our child was aborted, let us lay eggs which will be hatched long after we are dead.

We must live by the love of what we will never see. This is the secret of discipline. It is a refusal to let the creative act be dissolved away in immediate sense experience, and a stubborn commitment to the future of our grandchildren. Such disciplined love is what has given prophets, revolutionaries, and saints the courage to die for the future they envisaged. They made their own bodies the seed of their highest hope, because they knew that "a grain of wheat remains a solitary grain unless it falls into the ground and dies" (John 12:24).

Wake and listen,
you that are lonely!

From the future come winds with secret wing-beats;
and good-tidings are proclaimed to delicate ears.
You that are lonely today,
you that are withdrawing,
you shall one day be the people.
Verily, the earth shall yet become a site of recovery.
And even now a new fragrance surrounds it,
bringing salvation—and a new hope.[18]

18. Nietzsche, *Thus Spoke Zarathustra*, in Kaufmann, ed. *op. cit.*, p. 189.

Bibliography

Althusser, Louis. *For Marx*. New York: Vintage Books, 1970.

Berdyaev, Nikolai. *The Meaning of the Creative Act*. New York: Harper & Brothers, 1955.

_____. *Slavery and Freedom*. New York: Charles Scribners' Sons, 1944.

Berger, Peter. *Invitation to Sociology*. Garden City, N.Y.: Doubleday Anchor Books, 1963.

Berger, Peter, and Luckmann, Thomas. *The Social Construction of Reality*. Garden City, N.Y.: Doubleday & Co., 1967.

Bergson, Henri. *The Two Sources of Morality and Religion*. New York: Henry Holt & Co., 1935.

Bonhoeffer, Dietrich. *Letters and Papers from Prison*. London: SCM Press, 1953.

Brown, Norman O. *Life Against Death*. New York: Vintage Books, 1959.

Buber, Martin. *The Knowledge of Man*. London: George Allen & Unwin, 1965.

_____. *Paths in Utopia*. Boston: Beacon Press, 1958.

Campbell, H. J. "The Ultimate Pleasure." *New York Times*, April 14, 1971.

Camus, Albert. *The Rebel*. New York: Vintage Books, 1964.

Carroll, Lewis. *Alice's Adventures in Wonderland, Through the Looking Glass* and *The Hunting of the Snark*. New York: Boni & Liveright, 1924.

Cassirer, Ernst. *An Essay on Man*. Garden City, N.Y.: Doubleday & Co., 1953.

Dewey, John. *Art as Experience.* New York: Capricorn Books, 1958.

Durkheim, Émile. *The Elementary Forms of the Religious Life.* New York: Free Press, 1969.

Eisenstadt, S. N., ed. *Max Weber: On Charisma and Institution Building.* Chicago: University of Chicago Press, 1968.

Engels, Friedrich. *Feuerbach: The Roots of the Socialist Philosophy.* Chicago: Charles H. Kerr, 1912.

———. *Socialism: Utopian and Scientific.* Chicago: Charles H. Kerr & Co., n.d.

Escobar, Carlos Henrique, ed. *O Metodo Estruturalista.* Rio de Janeiro: Zahar, 1967.

Fanon, Frantz. *The Wretched of the Earth.* New York: Grove Press, 1968.

Feuerbach, Ludwig. *The Essence of Christianity.* New York: Harper & Brothers, 1957. *See also* Engels, Friedrich.

Freud, Sigmund. *Civilization and Its Discontents.* New York: W. W. Norton & Co., 1962.

———. *The Future of an Illusion.* Garden City, N.Y.: Doubleday & Co., 1964.

———. *Totem and Taboo.* New York: Vintage Books, 1946.

Fromm, Erich. *Marx's Concept of Man.* New York: Frederick Ungar Publishing Co., 1964.

Furter, Pierre. *Educação e Vida.* Petrópolis, Brasil: Vozes, 1968.

———. *L'Imagination Créatrice, la Violence et le Changement Social.* Cuernavaca, Mexico: Cidoc, 1968, Cuaderno 14.

Gerth, H. H., and Mills, C. Wright, eds. *From Max Weber, Essays in Sociology.* New York: Oxford University Press, 1946.

Goldenstein, Kurt. *The Organism.* Boston: Beacon Press, 1963.

Goodman, Paul. "La Mioralidad de la Tecnologia Cientifica." *Testimonium* XII.

———. *Utopian Essays and Practical Proposals.* New York: Random House, 1962.

Huizinga, Johan. *Homo Ludens.* Boston: Beacon Press, 1955.

Huxley, Aldous. *Brave New World.* New York: Harper & Brothers, 1946.

208   Tomorrow's Child

Jaeger, Gertrud, and Selznick, Phillip. "A Normative Theory of Culture," *American Sociological Review* (October 1964), p. 685.

Kaufmann, Walter. *Hegel: A Reinterpretation.* Garden City: N.Y.: Doubleday & Co., 1965.

Kaufmann, Walter, ed. *The Portable Nietzsche.* New York: Viking Press, 1968.

Kent, Corita. *Damn Everything but the Circus.* New York: Holt, Rinehart & Winston, 1970.

Kolakowski, Leszek. *Toward a Marxist Humanism.* New York: Grove Press, 1963.

Kroeber, Alfred L., and Parsons, Talcott. "The Concepts of Culture and of Social System," *American Sociological Review* (October 1958), p. 582.

Kuhn, Thomas S. *The Structure of Scientific Revolution.* Chicago: University of Chicago Press, 1966.

Lecky, Prescott. *Self-Consistency: A Theory of Personality.* Garden City, N.Y.: Doubleday & Co., 1961.

Lefebvre, Henri. *Le Langage et la Société.* Paris: Gallimard, 1966.

―――. "Reflexões sôbre o Estruturalismo e a História," *O Metodo Estruturalista*, Carlos Henrique Escobar, ed. (Rio de Janeiro: Zahar, 1967).

Lipset, S. M., and Wolin, S. S., eds. *The Student Berkeley Revolt: Facts and Interpretations.* Garden City, N.Y.: Doubleday Anchor Books, 1965.

Lukàcs, Georg. *Historia y Consciencia de Clase.* Mexico City: Grijalbo, 1969.

McLuhan, Marshall. *Understanding Media: The Extensions of Man.* New York: McGraw-Hill Book Co., 1964.

Malinowski, Bronislaw. *Magic, Science or Religion.* Boston: Beacon Press, 1948.

Mannheim, Karl. *Ideology and Utopia.* New York: Harcourt, Brace & Co., 1936.

Marx, Karl. *See* Althusser, Louis; Fromm, Erich.

Marx, Karl, and Engels, Friedrich. *The German Ideology.* New York: International Publishers, 1947.

_____. *On Religion*. New York: Schocken Books, 1964.

Masters, W. H., and Johnson, V. E. *Human Sexual Inadequacy*. Boston: Little, Brown & Co., 1970.

May, Rollo. *Man's Search for Himself*. New York: W. W. Norton & Co., 1953.

Merton, Robert K. *On Theoretical Sociology*. New York: Free Press, 1967.

Mumford, Lewis. *The Condition of Man*. New York: Harcourt, Brace & Co., 1944.

Musil, Robert. *The Man Without Qualities*. New York: Capricorn Books, 1965.

Myrdal, Gunnar. *An American Dilemma*. New York: Harper & Brothers, 1944.

Niebuhr, Reinhold. *Christian Realism and Political Problems*. New York: Charles Scribners' Sons, 1953.

Nietzsche, Friedrich. *See* Kaufmann, Walter, ed.

Orwell, George. *Nineteen Eighty-Four*. New York: Harcourt, Brace & Co., 1949.

Reich, Charles A. *The Greening of America*. New York: Bantam Books, 1971.

Roszak, Theodore. *The Making of a Counter-Culture*. Garden City, N.Y.: Doubleday & Co., 1969.

Rugg, Harold. *Imagination*. New York: Harper & Row, 1963.

Saint–Exupéry, Antoine de. *The Little Prince*. New York: Harcourt, Brace & World, Harbrace Paperbound Library, 1963.

Sartre, Jean Paul. *The Psychology of Imagination*. New York: Washington Square Press, 1968.

Scarf, Maggie. "Normality Is a Square Circle or a Four-Sided Triangle." *New York Times Magazine*, October 3, 1971.

Schwartz, Harry. "Forrester's Law." *New York Times*, June 14, 1971.

Stark, Werner. *The Sociology of Knowledge*. London: Routledge & Kegan Paul, 1967.

Stotland, Ezra. *The Psychology of Hope*. San Francisco: Jessy-Bas, 1969.

Tillich, Paul. *Political Expectation*. New York: Harper & Row, 1971.

Toffler, Alvin. *Future Shock*. New York: Random House, 1970.
Valéry, Paul. *Oeuvres*. La Pléiade, Paris: Gallimard, 1957.
Weber, Max. *See* Eisenstadt, S. N., ed.; Gerth, H. H. and Mills, C. Wright, eds.
Whitehead, Alfred N. *Science and the Modern World*. New York: Free Press, 1967.
Whyte, William H., Jr. *The Organization Man*. Garden City, N.Y.: Doubleday & Co., 1956.
Wittgenstein, Ludwig. *The Blue and Brown Books*. New York: Harper & Brothers, 1958.
———. *Tractatus Logico-Philosophicus*. New York: Humanities Press, 1961.

72 73 74 75 10 9 8 7 6 5 4 3 2 1

DATE DUE

F			
GAYLORD			PRINTED IN U.S.A.